Who Told You That You Were Naked?

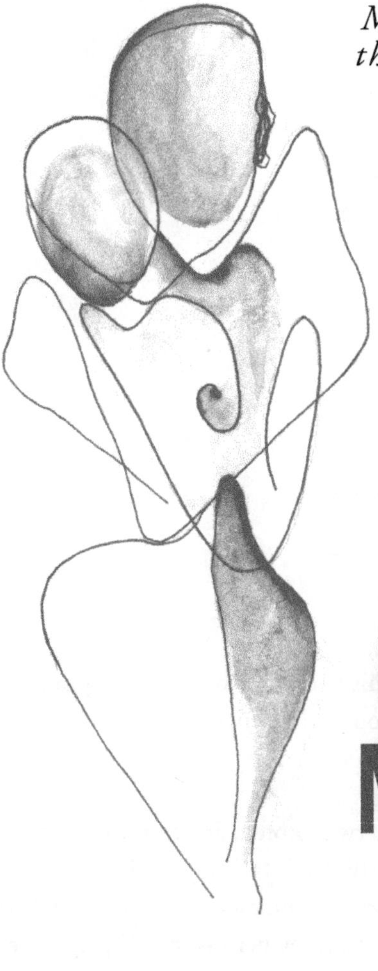

Meditations on the Sexual Body

WHO TOLD YOU THAT YOU WERE NAKED?

BEVERLY DALE

the pilgrim press

The Pilgrim Press, 1300 East 9th Street
Cleveland, Ohio 44114
thepilgrimpress.com

Published 2024.

Scripture quotations, unless otherwise noted, are from the New Revised Standard Version of the Bible, © 1989 by the Division of Christian Education of the National Council of Churches of Christ in the United States of America. Used by permission. Changes have been made for inclusivity.

Printed on acid-free paper.

Library of Congress Cataloging-in-Publication Data on file
Library of Congress Control Number: 2024930941

ISBN 978-0-8298-0080-7 (alk. paper)
ISBN 978-0-8298-0081-4 (ebook)

Printed in The United States of America.

DEDICATION

I dedicate this book to the healers among us:

- Pastors who teach liberation without condemnation,
- Therapists and counselors who accompany us with a vision for sexual well-being,
- Sex educators who combat harmful ignorance and promote health and healing,
- Theologians who dig for spiritual truths amidst cultural distortion,
- Teachers who open our minds,
- Friends who love, support, and challenge us.

May we together reconnect our bodies to our spirits and repair our broken world.

BEVERLY DALE
August 1, 2023

Nobody told me (Sex is Fun)[1]

Nobody told me that sex is fun.
Sex is fun!
Sex is fun!
They only told me that sex is sin.
Sex is sin!
Sex is sin!
We all know that sin is bad.
Sin is bad!
Sin is bad!
If fun is sin and sin is bad, then fun is bad.
Fun is bad!
Fun is bad!
If sex is fun and fun is sin, then sex is bad.
Sex is bad!
Sex is bad!
But we all know that sex is joy.
Sex is joy!
Sex is joy!
And we all know that God is joy.
God is joy!
God is joy!
If sex is joy and God is joy then sex is good.
Sex is good!
Sex is good!

Contents

Introduction

May my meditation be pleasing...

Psalm 104:34

For much of its history, major portions of traditional Christianity have maintained a disconnect between spirituality and sexuality, spirit and body. This has meant that for many, spirituality is experienced as asexual and experiences of the flesh are, too often, classified as sinful. Because of this suspicion towards sensuality and pleasure, rules, many of them unwritten, emerged early on to allow only a narrow range of "appropriate" sensual or sexual experiences for believers. The result is that many Christians have learned to downplay that we are sexual beings; meanwhile, consistently negative messaging and the absence of a positive connection between the life of the Spirit as accessed through bodily, enfleshed, sensual experiences promote shame of the sexual body. This shame at our sexual feelings and choices makes us afraid of our erotic selves and instills deep guilt. Shame also pressures us to conform to others' rules about who we can be attracted to, how we must present in society's gender roles, and our relationship lifestyle choices. Few understand that the restrictions and erotophobic teachings we hear from preachers and priests, vote-seeking politicians, or family members do not, in fact, come from the life or the teachings of Jesus. Period. They are not to be found in the gospel stories of Jesus. Repeat: They *are not found* in the gospels.

Regardless, just as the earth creatures did in Eden, too many of us cower before the Creator with ridiculously useless fig leaves to hide, control, or repress our nakedness. But hiding behind fig leaves is not consistent with the first creation story in Genesis 1. There, all of creation is pronounced "very good." Presumably, this includes all of our beautifully varied bodies with all of our wild fantasies and our variety of bodily needs, sexual desires, and diversities.

It is imperative then that we jettison body shaming, our suspicion of pleasure, the moralistic and judgmental repression of both our own sexuality and that of others, as well as the many forms of harmful sex-negativity currently contaminating some areas of Christian thought. We are destroying our sexual self-esteem and damaging our intimate relationships. In truth, much of the systemic harm of physical injustice in the global family is a result of the dis-ease towards things carnal and pleasurable that emerged through Western thought and Christian teaching. But our religious views on the sexual body can be deconstructed and separated from the gospel of Jesus. By decoupling this negativity, we can keep our faith as Christians, if we so choose.

The first step toward sexual liberation is to develop a spiritual practice that includes body-positive teaching. What follows in this book is such a practice. It contains meditations and reflections that include scripture, prayer, and activities to assist in breaking away from sexual guilt, body shame, and the fear of judgment about our sexuality. Each one is designed to provoke thinking that affirms this aspect of our humanity, embraces diversity of bodily experience, and, without judgment, validates our needs and desires in a way designed to heal any negativity we have learned and stored in our bodies. The goal is to move us toward sexual liberation and a faithfully moral sexual ethic.

These meditations are guided by the wisdom of scripture, the foundation for Christian living. Biblical stories and texts open us to an understanding of what it is to be human and offer guidance toward righteous living. Seeking deeper spiritual understanding of how we are to live and love sexually and sensually requires that we reflect upon and grapple with biblical texts and traditional interpretations. Each meditation and the reflection activities that follow are also guided by the insights of scientific research about what constitutes sexual health and well-being. As such, although these disciplines ask different questions, the book aims to keep Christian teaching in dialogue with science. Ultimately, both science and Christianity seek health and healing and are interested in enhancing the well-being of humanity. Practitioners in the field of sexual science engage with research on how to support positive self-esteem in individuals as well as healthy intimate relationships that are unencumbered by sexual guilt, body shame and fear. Christianity says the well-being of humanity is found in an abundant and liberating life following the Teacher in Galilee who, as God-in-the-Flesh, exhibits an inclusive love for all.

Each meditation concludes with a prayer that intentionally avoids using the metaphor that often enforces sexual guilt and body shame: Father God. For too many, this metaphor denotes a white, angry, vengeful, and judgmental Being who has a dim opinion of sexual behavior or erotic feelings. By freeing ourselves to employ more creative metaphors we can more easily move into a liberating space of sexual freedom.

Following each meditation is an opportunity for reflection that consists of two to five activities, thought experiments, and journal invitations intended to invite a personal response. These reflective activities will plumb the feelings and memories that arise and provide a way to acknowledge, refute, and release any harmful messages. Since many of our memories and insights are stored in the body, some reflections include movement and physical actions. This allows us to access and release that which is harmful and to restore and affirm healing messages linked to the insights from the meditations.

Keeping a journal is highly recommended to honor the thoughts and feelings, memories and tensions that will be part of the process, including new questions and spiritual understandings that will, no doubt, arise.

The call of this book is to release ourselves from all sex negativity with its guilt and shame and to consider instead what sexual freedom might look like through an ethical rather than a moralistic lens. First, however, we must lose our fear of both the judgmental punishment of the Divine and the potential ostracism of the church. This is a challenge to be sure. However, a better focus for our spiritual and sexual journey would be the discovery of the sexual ethics of a righteous life as we live into our sexual freedom as people of faith. Rather than repression, what would happen if we loved and took delight and pleasure in our divinely created bodies? How would this change the way we interact with others? If we were comfortable in our own sensual skin, how would it change our view of those unlike us? If we followed Jesus's example, then would our lives not begin to resemble the abundant life he both taught and lived (John 10:10)?

HOW TO READ THESE MEDITATIONS AND REFLECTIONS

Some conservative Christian traditions focus on body restrictions and expect uniformity, agreement, and obedience to a set of sexual norms. This is not such a rule book, nor should readers expect to find easy answers or a one-size-fits-all approach about how to live in sexual freedom as people of faith. We are glorious in our differences according to scripture (1 Corinthians 12) and, just as our spiritual gifts are different, so our spiritual paths will vary. The author is a white, educated, middle-class, able-bodied ordained

Christian clergy from the United States who is a cis-gender, heterosexual grandmother. Thus, these meditations reflect the wisdom from this unique social location and her own spiritual journey toward sexual wholeness. Many factors influence how each reader will experience these meditations. The racialized colors of our skin, the places of our birth, our class differences and differently abled bodies, as well as how we approach gender, gender identities, and roles all combine with our various sexual traumas, personal pain, and bodily experiences.

It is no surprise, then, that since life happens to each reader differently, so we grow and thrive in our Christian faith in a variety of ways. Thus, our spiritual pathways are different. With the guidance of the Holy Spirit, we can be certain that if we seek, we shall find (Luke 8:9–10) and when we knock on the door of Wisdom it will be opened to us regardless of those differences. Note that it is Wisdom that we seek, not a one-size-fits-all sexual standard. The major underlying assumption of this book is that the One who holds us in love can and will guide each one of us through the quagmire of centuries of erotophobic Christian and Western cultural teaching that have split our bodies from our spirits.

Thus, the reader should approach each meditation asking whether or not the Spirit is teaching an important truth for their own life. If it is not, simply move to another one. Remain open, and "if there is any excellence and if there is anything worthy of praise, think about these things" (Philippians 4:8).

To be clear, healing the split between our bodies and spirits can be difficult—and painful. At times, memories and feelings related to alienation or abuse, to poor decisions or traumatic events can surface. These meditations and reflections may serve as a trigger and catalyst for additional healing even as they are a trigger for those painful memories and feelings. There are resources in the appendix to further consider the breath of body injustice that intimately connects sexuality to the color of our skin, our finances, health issues, and other factors of our bodily experience. However, this work is not intended to be nor can it be a substitute for professional assistance. It is recommended that you seek professional counselors or therapists with academic training in sexuality and sexual health research with perhaps certification with the American Association of Sex Educators, Counselors and Therapists (AASECT) should the work that follows trigger those painful feelings and memories for you. In addition, some trained professionals have received additional science-friendly, faith-based training in sexuality and Christianity from the Incarnation Institute for Sex & Faith (IISF).

IN THE BEGINNING THERE WAS A GARDEN

According to a certain biblical worldview, the story of humanity begins in a beautiful and sensual Garden of Earthly Delights named Eden where the first earth creatures "were naked and not ashamed" (Genesis 1:25). In the very beginning, so the story goes, they are innocent. Intimately connected with the Divine, they understand neither life nor death, good nor evil. Those secrets are held in the fruit of two trees,[2] one of which they choose to eat. After this act, they understand that life is complicated: they now see a distinction between the creation and the Creator. This new awareness replaces their innocence, leaving them feeling vulnerable. And, then as now, vulnerability makes us want to cover ourselves and hide. That is what those first earth creatures did with fig leaves.

Yet the Creator called them, and calls us, out from those hiding places. There is no need to hide when we feel separated. We are still made in the Creator's image and still created to live in a beautiful and sensual Garden of Earthly Delights. We can still live in and with Love while in these human bodies. The creation can still stand unashamed before the Creator, laying aside the construct of our separation. After all, from the Creator's viewpoint, neither the first humans nor we ourselves have ever been separated. In fact, the Creator demands to know: who told us that we are separated? Where did we learn that we had to cover ourselves in shame to hide naked vulnerability? Who says that the very essence of being human in all our sensual and sexual earthiness is forbidden? It wasn't the Creator! And, yet, here we remain, thousands of years later, still covered in shame and guilt, feeling that to be sexual is problematic for the spiritual life. It is quite possible that the Creator is still standing before us demanding to know, "Who told you that you were naked?" (3:11)

The core teaching of Christianity is incarnation - that God dwells in the flesh, both in Jesus but also in the Body of Christ that is comprised of all Christians. Sometimes we call this indwelling the Holy Spirit. Understood outside the lens of Christianity, it is living into the image of the Divine while knowing that the Light of God burns in each of us. Sometimes it is experiencing the Sacred when we connect with one another in the work of justice-making or in the play of safely loving and sharing our bodies. The purpose of these meditations and reflections is to help us return to being "naked and unashamed" (Genesis 2:25) just like the first earth creatures in the Garden. When we are unashamed of our vulnerability and nakedness, we can find our way back to the Sacred within these bodies. It is from this Divine Center that we "live and move and have our being" as the apostle Paul proclaimed (Acts 17:28). But until we reconnect this goodness to our own sexual and sensual bodies, we will not be able to recognize our sacred home to which we are always welcome, and which was intended from the beginning to be experienced as a Garden of Earthly Delights. This is where we are at home, in a place of Oneness where the Divine

Source is Overwhelming Joy, Abundant Life, and Everlasting Love. Our goal is to come home to ourselves and to our source. Then, standing without shame in these sacred vessels of beautiful sexual and sensual bodies we will hear, "Welcome home!"

part one

The Purity Culture

Perfection or Authenticity?

Think On these Things

God's temple is holy, and you are that temple.

1 Corinthians 3:17

Just as there are two sides of a coin, when we think about our bodies as sexual, there can be two unhelpful sides of some Christian views about bodies. They are either sinful *or* they must be pure; one lives in irresponsible hedonism *or* in spiritual perfection. The focus is reduced to either an obsession with sex *or* obedience to restrictions on sexual behaviors and thoughts, fantasies, and needs. These views limit who we are as sexual beings because the attention is primarily directed toward the genitalia—what, when, and where they are or want to be! What might be more helpful for our spiritual and sexual lives is to ask what is potentially harmful to ourselves or others and what is authentic to the inner callings of the Spirit and of an ethic of love.? In other words, what is spiritually enhancing versus what is spiritually damaging? What is the way the Spirit moves us toward righteousness versus the way others think we should move? This shifts the attention away from the physicality of genitalia to the spirituality of the body that includes the heart and soul as well. According to the Hebrew prophets, the authors of the Christian scripture, and Jesus's teachings, *this* is where God is focused—on the intention of the action rather than the action divorced from its source, on the heart rather than the body parts, on the life as it is lived rather than the life as it is denied, stifled, or repressed.

Unfortunately, traditional Christian teaching rarely ponders how pleasure and play, sensual delight and joy in our bodies connect to spirituality. But the more pleasure we experience, create, and share, the more gratitude we feel for the sacred gift of life and the more spontaneous praise arises at the divinely inspired wonder of it all. Rather than considering the flesh as sexual (read: bad) and spirit as asexual (read: good), we would do well to ask ourselves how our fleshly senses are or can be channels or doorways to the creator. For when we connect more fully to our own bodies we can connect more fully with the bodies of others and with the divine.

Yet, as we move toward a body-affirming spirituality, another dichotomy becomes apparent: God-as-Judge versus God-as-Lover. This is the glue that tightly holds sex-negativity in place. When it comes to our bodies and sexuality, many Christians have accented God as a Judge who leans more toward harshness than tolerance, more toward judgment than compassion, more toward reserve than play. In other words, God as Judge sits frowning from the sidelines rather than cheering us on from the thick of life's game with us. By investing in this image of God, we risk separating our spiritual lives from our sensual selves instead of deeply integrating them. While judgment-making and loving are certainly not mutually exclusive, an overemphasis on this image of God as Judge may lead to a failure to accentuate the idea of God as Lover…and, specifically, a lover of our sexual bodies. With God-as-Judge, it is easy to believe that one is faced with the choice of either striving for obedience or risking being caught-in-the-act and guilty-as-charged criminals! In an understanding of ourselves as seeking to be obedient children of God, we may well strive for perfection to avoid punishment and to gain parental reward—perhaps even favored child status. Any sense of ourselves as guilt-ridden and disobedient could bring a focus on the severe penalty we anticipate for being caught as sexual humans.

Yet, taking Jesus as our model helps to reveal this image of God-as-Judge to be a distortion. Jesus did not sit on the sidelines pronouncing judgment on the masses for their earthly experiences, nor did Jesus avoid the sensuality of life. And although there were ascetics who denied their physical needs during his day, he did not participate in that lifestyle. Instead, the gospel portrays him as someone who cared deeply for those around him and who moved easily among a wide variety of people. He talked and joked with intellectuals and professionals, children and women, the sick and the lowly with no judgment for their state of health, their scabs and smells, their dirt and poverty or wealth, or their gendered selves as eunuchs or females. The stories reveal that he attended boisterous feasts and sumptuous banquets, told stories, went fishing on the Sea of Galilee, and grilled the latest catch on the beach all while being authentically human.

Might we then say that all attempts to denigrate our human bodies as somehow tainted or sinful violates the church's central message of Jesus as God-in-the-flesh? It contradicts the intertwining of spiritual and physical in his existence that is evident in the church's own conclusion that Jesus was "fully human and fully divine." Further, it is an affront to the thoughtfulness of the Creator who gave us body parts with no function except pleasure.

If the central story of the Christian church is Jesus as the Incarnation of God (John 1:14), then we must rebalance the image of the Divine. This will enable us to live fully and authentically into our humanity without apology, just as Jesus did.

Think on these things as you read the following meditations on perfection and authenticity.

- How fleshly are you allowed to be?
- How can flesh also be spirit?
- Who is the focus if we seek perfection?
- What would a "pure" Christian look like relative to the body?
- How easy would it be to consider the "Great I Am" as your intimate lover who longs for good things for you?

"The World"

MEDITATION

You have heard it said . . . but I say to you . . .

Matt 5:21–22, 27–28, 33–34, 43–44

We conform and perform as a way of life often without questioning the impact this has on our bodies: Exhaustion. Stress. Anxiety. Fear. Isolation. They all seem normal, but when normality needs to be reexamined, Jesus said: "You have heard it said . . . but I say to you . . ." Similarly, the apostle Paul contrasted the ways of "the world" (often translated "the flesh") with the ways of the Spirit. The glitter of the "world" keeps us distracted, so the priority becomes the superficial "self-care" of the individual rather than the thriving of a joy-filled, righteous community. "The world," as Paul used the term, is a system of oppression that keeps the machinery of commerce, war, and politics operating by separating us from the energy of joy and pleasure found in our bodies.

The mind control of "the world" is exhausting. It says, "Your body is defective. You need to buy something to make it more presentable." And, "True happiness and purpose come with material success, so you have to work harder." It does not matter if the price is insufficient time with our children or little time for relaxing or socializing with friends or if it fragments community. Just as important, if we truly lived a sensual, joy-filled life focused on a sense of deep pleasure, we would never allow or participate in those cultural practices nor obey laws that prevent others from experiencing their own joy-filled life. In a system of domination, pleasure always takes a back seat to productivity. Productivity cannot abide joy and play is never allowed. This is the mind control of "the world."

Reconnecting the flesh to our spirituality and playfully relishing pleasure are revolutionary acts. Joy begets joy. To refuse to allow death-dealing rules of "the world" to control our minds by minimizing the truth of our bodies is to follow in the footsteps of the one who said, "Follow me." And that message changes lives and could transform the world.

World-changer, we cry out for deliverance when we see and feel the death-dealing ways of the world. We grow tired of other people's rules and endlessly conforming to the ways of the world just to survive. What happened to joy? Why mindless routines? Why are we separated from one another? With these bodies we can see you, feel you, and know you yet, too often, we shut out and shut down possibilities for this joy. Open us to the experiences of pleasure we knew as children. Then, we can change our life and the world, one joyful experience at a time.

REFLECTION

1. When we experience a mind/body split, both our bodies and our minds are more easily controlled. Think about a time in which you made a decision that brought you weariness and stress and denied your own bodily desires.
    a. What price did you pay?
    b. Did you get a reward? Was it sufficient?
    c. Do you habitually make sacrifices that deny yourself time for pleasure?
2. What change do you need to instigate in your life that would give you more joy? And what would you need to jettison to

make it happen? Write it in your journal and make a small step to move in that direction.

3. Experiential activity: Do an internal self-assessment of your body right now. How comfortable are you in your body? Do you feel any twinges, discomfort, or pain? Now listen to what your body's wisdom tells you that you need. Then, breathing slowly and deeply, move into positions that will be helpful. As you become more aware of your body's wisdom to seek comfort, begin to use your breath as sighs of relief. Let every breath of relief say, "Thank you for your wisdom." Listen carefully because once your body has your attention, it may request movement or activity that would be fun or that would feel good. Listen. Do it.

Growing in Faith, Stuck in Obedience

MEDITATION

We must no longer be children . . . we must grow up in every way.

Ephesians 4:14

Although the cause is still medically unclear, running and jumping vigorously through the day might explain why some children experience growing pains in their legs and thighs at night. Adults have "growing" pains too, perhaps not physically, but certainly spiritually. This is when we are filled with questions and doubts that can plunge us into a time of spiritual disquiet. Growing pains of faith often occur in the movement from being a child-like obedient Christian to an autonomously discerning one. It requires spiritual discernment over time. The goal is not to arrive at spiritual maturity but to stay on the path that moves us toward it. It is not to shrug off all rules but to determine which ones are best for our own lives. As every parent of a teenager recognizes, the shift from obeying parental rules to deciding what is right for themselves takes time and can be difficult, if not painful. Emotional maturity for adolescents includes that recognition. While it can be especially hurtful to hear those we trust imply that they know more about what is right for us than we do ourselves, this can signal our growing ability to claim our own moral agency that is a sign of growth. Shifting from obeying to growing can feel confusing because we are torn between loyalty to the rule keepers or enforcers and our desire to truly follow God's will. Rather than obeying other people's rules without discernment, listen to trusted friends as well as the Spirit Within even while grappling with scripture and church teaching. People of faith listen, discern, and, with or without growing pains, discover how to live in their bodies as God desires and as fits their needs.

Wisdom Within, help us hear your voice amidst all the confusion. Teach us to trust in your Spirit that is always nearby showing us how to love in your name. Keep us from obeying rules just to keep the peace or to fit in. Just as children grow into their own individuality, teach us to honor the gift of our unfolding wisdom about sexuality. You do not condemn questions and doubts nor does our growing and changing threaten you. And should we go in the wrong direction, call us back to your side.

REFLECTION

1. Make a list of three actions that parents may think children absolutely must obey. Then identify three rules some parents might impose that are out of sync with the developmental

stage of the child and that, although perhaps reassuring to the parent, may thus inhibit the emotional growth of the child.

2. Identify three rules from your youth that you resented or rebelled against. How did you feel? Was there a wisdom in the rule? Was there a wisdom in your resentment and rebellion?
3. Name a time when you obeyed someone else's rules even though it didn't feel right for you. How did that make you feel?
4. Read this affirmation aloud:

It's okay to challenge others' rules about my body
    it means I am growing
It's okay to grow and change
    it means I'm finding my own way.
It's okay to decide for myself
    it means I am building myself up in love.
It's okay to make mistakes and to be uncertain
    it means I'll soon find my way.

Now repeat two more times and note any hesitation you may have.

The Perfection of Authenticity

MEDITATION

The fruit of the Spirit is love, joy, peace, patience, kindness, generosity, faithfulness, gentleness, and self-control.

Galatians 5:22–23

The love of God has reached perfection.

1 John 4:5

One way to control sexuality is to hold an ideal of perfection. "The world" has its own version of perfection; glorifying the "perfect" body type and giving higher status to a "perfect" lifestyle of thin (white) women and buff (white) men who practice heterosexual monogamy with 2.5 children in the suburbs. Not coincidentally, the world's "perfection" requires spending money on Botox, cosmetics, weight-loss programs, gym memberships, and the latest fashions. Yet the church idolizes the idea of perfection when it tries to control sexual expression and diversity and creates rules of self-giving sacrifice—primarily to women—implying there is such a thing as sexual purity in scripture. The concept of sexual purity as it has evolved in the context of contemporary purity culture is absent from the text of the Bible. We forget that if the Creator had wanted perfection, we would all be angelic beings instead of human beings.

Trying to be "perfect" and live by perfectionistic standards that include denial and repression of our human sexual needs can easily lead to guilt and shame, game-playing and hypocrisy, rather than joyful, authentic living. The philosopher Socrates taught that "to find yourself, think for yourself." So, think on these things: Jesus taught that we are to be righteous in thought and deed. The apostle

Paul defined righteousness as producing fruits of the spirit: love, joy, peace, patience, kindness, generosity, faithfulness, gentleness, and self-control (Galatians 5:22–23), but especially love (1 Corinthians 13:8, 13). Righteousness cannot be reduced to a listing of good deeds to do and bad deeds not to do with our sexual bodies. Rather, let us consider the possibility of God's boundless love based on who we are. Just as we are. After all, righteousness is not contingent upon the number of mistakes or bad decisions we may or may not make. God's abundant Love frees us to live authentically, accepting who we are as sensual and sexual creatures made in the image of the Divine. This is not the image of perfection but the image of Goodness and Love. And that is just perfect!

O Wondrous Love, forgive us when we attempt to be someone we are not nor were ever even made to be. Forgive us for the times we fail to simply be ourselves because we fear moralistic judgment, whether our own, yours, or others. Help us to discover our authentic selves so we can live with integrity in all our choices unconcerned about the standards others may hold. We celebrate that your only standard is love. Help us begin by loving ourselves.

REFLECTION

1. Being authentic requires that we are honest and accepting of ourselves, like God is of us. Can you identify some of the ways it is difficult to be honest about your sexuality? About your body? Then, write a prayer of gratitude for your unique self.
2. Identify the people or situations where you may fear being your true and authentic self.
3. Mirror exercise: Find a mirror and tell your image the following phrases aloud:

"I am loved just as I am. I am not perfect but the Creator doesn't expect perfection." (Repeat three times.)

"I am worthy just as I am. I am not perfect but God doesn't expect perfection." (Repeat three times.)

4. Journaling exercise: How did you feel when you said these phrases? What feelings were churned up for you? Was it easy to do? If it was not, identify the voice in your head as "The Inner Critic." Write a letter in your journal to "The Inner Critic" to acknowledge that, while they may think they are being helpful or protecting you, from now on, you will no longer be listening to them. Inasmuch as this "Critic" lives rent free in our minds, disinvite them from that residence.

The Perfection of Being Different

MEDITATION

There are many members, yet one body.

1 Corinthians 12:20

Human beings may have an innate survival instinct to seek out people who are like us; those who think, sound, and look like us. The primitive urge may arise out of insecurity and fear of those creatures, human or animal, who are different and therefore potentially dangerous. Our primal instinct that says uniformity helps us to survive made sense when we lived in the wild; it is wrong-headed when we live in community. Uniformity may keep the peace, but it does not help us survive.

The key to survival is biodiversity. Diverse ecosystems are far superior to monocultures. We have discovered that with all our differences, we still breathe the same air, rely on the same water, and that our survival as a species and planetary system depends on all of us surviving together. Similarly, research[3] shows that diverse groups of people are far better problem-solvers than homogenous groups. This means we must become comfortable with our differences and recognize that the more diverse perspectives we can learn about and incorporate into our lives, the better informed and more adaptive we become. Rather than being fearful, it is when we are curious about differences that our world expands and we find ourselves opening up to new possibilities that isolated stances simply cannot reveal.

Our human diversity mirrors a wildly diverse creation. All this wondrous diversity on the planet and in humanity is awaiting our joyful discovery.

And the more we learn, the more humility we develop. The more we accept diversity as a fact of nature, the more we accept, value, and build on the strengths of our differences. Then we can solve our mutual problems together. That is the gift of diversity. It is the gift of sexual diversity as well.

Dear Creative One, thank you for the boundless multitude of creatures and the magnificent variety in our world. We are blessed even as this sometimes makes us afraid. Help us replace our fear of difference with curiosity. Forgive us for trying to make others in our own image and teach us to accept others' unique paths. Then, may we in humility remember that in all our diversity, each one of us is seen by your watchful eye and covered by your grace. Thank you.

REFLECTION

1. Name an animal or a plant that seems so outrageously strange and different or novel that it gives you delight or wonder.
2. Name three things about yourself that make you unique.
3. As a child, when did you first notice that people were different? What messages about difference did you receive from those around you?
4. What sexual differences among people are troublesome to you or cause you to fear? Consider who might help you understand and accept sexual diversity as God-created.
5. Repeat the following affirmations:

   I may be different from others in some ways
   Yet, I am made in the image of God.
   I am unique and one of a kind
   Yet, so is everyone else.
   In a unique and homogenous world, I can feel safe
   Yet, in God's diverse world I can flourish
   Inside my comfort zone I rest, heal, and rejuvenate
   Yet, outside my comfort zone is energy, creativity, and wonder.
   I vow to be open to others.
   I vow to be curious about differences.
   I vow to appreciate the wonder, awe, and goodness of
   my diverse world.

The Perfection of Our "Imperfection"

MEDITATION

Whoever fears has not reached perfection in love.

1 John 4:18

Jesus never taught that we should lay aside biologically driven desires, sexual or otherwise, nor did he teach that we should avoid sensual pleasure or deny the human sensual need for caresses. Yet, these desires for touch, intimacy, and pleasure are often condemned through the "purity" teachings of the conservative church. When this is interwoven with our fear of being judged, especially with divine punishment, we may give up our own agency and depend on someone else's standards, whether it be a pastor, our church, or an image of God, which may feel moralistically judgmental. This interweaving also connects sexuality and sin in a highly suspect way and, inevitably, instills guilt, fear, and shame.

Driven by fear and the need for approval, we may seek "sexual purity" even though God seeks righteous living. We are not expected to seek some state of perfection but rather faithfulness. We delight God when our lives are guided by righteous sexual decision-making and loving respect in all our intimate interactions. Such a standard would more closely imitate the life and teachings of Jesus.

Presbyterian pastor Fred Rogers had a life-affirming mantra for the children who watched his television show, *Mr. Rogers' Neighborhood*. It was "I love you just the way you are." This simple message for the child in all of us summarizes God's abundant grace and unending love. Our true perfection comes when we release fear and get lost in love. The lyricist Charlotte Elliott glimpsed this love when writing the hymn, "Just As I Am." For her, God's love welcomes, pardons, cleanses, and relieves. Love invites us to lay down the burdens of guilt and shame and jump into the swirling waters of God's total acceptance just as we are: sexual and sensual beings. Released from our fears of never-good-enough, we can float on the rhythms of God's murmuring voice: "I love you just the way you are." And, "I will never abandon or forsake you" (Hebrews 13:5).

O Lover God, we can't begin to understand that your love can overlook and forgive all our imperfections especially when we can hardly forgive ourselves. Forgive us when we cling to unworthiness rather than simply living in the perfection of your love. Remind us of your love so that we may begin to believe it, share it, live it, and finally to become it.

REFLECTION

1. Name any body-negative messages you received. Who gave you those messages? Were they verbally or non-verbally conveyed? Make a list of those people, places, and situations where these messages were conveyed either intentionally or inadvertently. And then do the following exercise either as a thought experiment or physically by using pieces of paper and placing them in an envelope:

   a. Imagine each item on your list is an entity that can be folded and put into a large envelope. Now state each name, place, or situation as you imagine inserting it into an envelope.

   b. As you do so, read aloud the following:

      I dismiss this message from my life. You no longer have the power to repeat your message. It is harmful. It is wrong. You do not have the power to hurt me again.

I send you far away from my world. I send you to the hands of God.
I shall heal. I shall be whole. I shall be loving to my beautiful, sensual, and sexual body.

c. Then, either imagine or physically destroy the envelope as you repeat the last line.

   I shall heal.
   I shall be whole.
   I shall be loving to my beautiful, sensual, and sexual body.

2. To hang onto the sense that we are never going to meet some standard of perfection is a form of pride. It means, "I am so shameful or bad or unworthy that no one can possibly love me, or forgive me, or accept me." Consider how many times would you have to hear this statement before you actually believe it:

   "I love you just the way you are."

   And now, go to a mirror and start repeating it until you reach that number.

The Perfection of Miraculous Bodies

MEDITATION

I am fearfully and wonderfully made. Wonderful are your works.

Psalm 139:14

Too many Christians focus on sexual purity and obsess on their failure to attain some level of perfection. That is in part because we are stuck seeing the sexual body in an absolute sinful state rather than as the miracle it is. Our bodies are amazingly intricate and, as the most important sex organ in our bodies, the brain sends nerve impulses to and from the brain at 170 miles per hour so we can react to sexual initiation at the speed of a high-powered sports car! The bonding chemical oxytocin is an endorphin that peaks during orgasm at five times its usual level and numbs raw nerve endings. It eases migraines and arthritis pain. Blood cells shoot from the heart at rest at one mile an hour and complete the full circle of our circulatory system in only thirty seconds while, in thirty minutes alone, the average body gives off enough heat to boil a half gallon of water. And, a too-often overlooked but sexually significant fact is that the clitoris has eight thousand nerve endings, twice the number found on the head of the penis.

Regarding our bodies as miraculous allows us to dismiss criticisms and limitations as the illusions they are. Our perfect imperfections deserve respectful attention, loving care, and protection from harm. All denigrations of bodies due to size, age, form, class, race, abilities, gender, or orientation come from arrogance and ignorance, whether that criticism is from an internal or external voice. The Creator is not a liar when pronouncing all of creation and our diverse bodies as "very good." Bodies are not meant to be "perfect," but are, in fact, perfectly miraculous.

O Miracle Maker, we praise you that miraculous bodies work so well without the requirement of forethought, planning, or oversight. Forgive us when we take them for granted or are inattentive to our body's needs. Remind us that it is an affront to you when we hear criticism or condemnation of our bodies, needs, or desires. For, we have wonderfully and fearfully made sexual bodies.

REFLECTION

1. Experiential Activity: The Miracle of Hands

For five minutes, focus on the miracle of your hands as they rest in your lap. First examine your hands and the map of veins and arteries that can be seen and felt. Using the index finger of one hand, trace this map on your other hand and consider the miracle of the fast-moving blood just beneath the surface. Turn your hand over to look at the palm and the folds of skin that conveniently allow it to open and close. Open and close your hand. Examine any callouses or scars that might reflect your labors or show past encounters, surgeries, or accidents. Lift and wiggle each finger and consider the number of muscles under the skin. Try to move each finger horizontally, toward the other hand and away from it. Watch how some fingers move more easily than others. Now allow your hands to float upward to dance in the air, slowly, carefully, gracefully. Make circles and figures, then move quickly as if your hands are taking flight with the birds. Next, slow down and stroke your hand as a lover might to indicate how very special and miraculous you are. Hands can be helpful, lifting and assisting others. Rest your hands in your lap without moving. Remember they convey kindness, give comfort, and bring gifts. Your hands are amazing. Why? Because they are yours. Hands are miracles and they are part of your miraculous body.

2. Affirmation: Repeat the following sentences aloud twice.

This body is a miracle. I am a miracle. (Repeat)
My body is a miraculous vessel. It houses my spirit. (Repeat)
I am more than my body but my body is an expression of my spirit. (Repeat)

My spirit is seen through the actions of this miraculous vessel. (Repeat)
May I live in gratitude. (Repeat)
May I live inside this miracle. (Repeat)
May I spread joy. (Repeat)

The Perfection of Our Beauty

MEDITATION

Mortals . . . look on the outward appearance,
but the Lord looks on the heart.

1 Samuel 19:26

"You are very pretty . . ." These complimentary words from my mother to my insecure fifteen-year-old self were lovely to hear yet were immediately nullified by the following phrase, "but, you must never believe that." In her Christian upbringing, there was no greater sin than pride and vanity, especially for women. Unfortunately, some Christian thought, while anti-body, is obsessed with the body's appearance, believing that our weight or shape is comparable to sin. This idea connects our outward appearance as a sign of faith or godliness. As a result, how we look can take priority over how we act. There is nothing inherently sinful or ugly about these bodies of ours with all our shapes, colors, sizes, or abilities because they are divinely created and beautifully formed miracles. Every. Single. One. Of. Us. We should not worry about restricting or enhancing the body because this inherent miracle given by the Creator is not to be confused with the outward fashion of the world.

Whether we are controlling our vanity to suppress sexual responses or whether we are controlling appearances to conform to some supposed godly standard of beauty, both shift us away from the heart, which is where God is focusing (1 Samuel 19:26). It is our heart that spurs us toward actions that come through our bodies. For the sixteenth-century Christian mystic Teresa of Avila, it is our bodies that channel the Christ. She wrote, "Yours are the feet with which Christ walks to do good. Yours are the hands with which Christ blesses the world. Yours are the eyes through which Christ looks [with] compassion into the world." God uses these fabulously made bodies to spread love and justice into a sexually wounded world that simply does not understand what Love looks like. And, sometimes, we forget too.

God of our beautiful hearts, bring us back to the quiet places where we hear your whispers of love, where we feel your arms surrounding our physical bodies with acceptance and grace. Quiet the loud din that screams that our bodies are insufficient and lacking. Quiet the sounds of self-criticism. Help us screen out the condemning standards that focus on the external but neglect the heart. Inhabit our hearts instead so that your grace may flow through these bodies.

REFLECTION

1. If someone ever implied you were not beautiful, write a paragraph detailing the memory. Read it aloud, allowing yourself to feel whatever comes. Gently remind yourself it was/is a lie. Now imagine a child standing before you who has told you this painful story. Write a loving response. If you are writing in longhand, use your non-dominant hand and let compassion flow through you as you help the child to heal from the pain.[4]

2. Experiential activity: Cross your arms in front of your body with your palms on your chest and fingers pointed upward at your shoulder blades in what is known as a "butterfly kiss." Gently pat yourself with your fingers. In this posture, slowly reread the prayer on the preceding page, feeling the warm and loving pats on your body. Hear the whispers of love for you and your beautiful body. And if you feel any resistance and internal criticism, imagine a door closing gently against such sounds. Enjoy the peace and quiet of self-acceptance. Be in the moment and feel your heart quietly beating. Breathe in grace. "All is well. And all will be well."[5]
3. Experiential activity: What one thing do you wish someone had told you about the miraculous beauty of your body? Write it ten times, adding your name each time. Using colorful markers or crayons, create a poster to prominently display this affirmation. If you wish, sign it as a divine message: "Love, God of Your Beautiful Heart."

Deceit and the Sunglasses Test

MEDITATION

The heart is deceitful above all things,
and desperately wicked: who can know it?

Jeremiah 17:9[6]

Sometimes the world changes color depending on which pair of sunglasses we wear; one pair casts a light bluish gray shade while another reflects greenish yellow. Our biblical "sunglasses" are colored by our culture and personal experiences, which shape how we approach life, see God, and read the Bible. Our personal "sunglasses" are affected by whether there was an abundance of love in our childhood or multiple encounters of unloving relationships or only conditional acceptance. These experiences will affect whether we see life as a glass half empty or half full. Our perspective (sunglasses) and past experiences determine whether we see life positively or negatively. If we see abundance in a half-full glass, we will behave in more assertive, courageous, and risk-taking ways. But if we see scarcity in a half-empty one, we may live in survival mode instead.

To put this in religious language, God says, "I set before you life or death. Choose life." (Deuteronomy 30:19) The two driving forces in our spiritual lives are the power of love and the power of fear. A focus on scarcity will easily move us into fear. The above translation of Jeremiah 17:9 that asserts we have deceitful hearts is consistent with this scarcity view and is often equated with judgment against us for being sexual creatures who always choose sin. When we lay aside this Western perspective for which the nature of humanity is deplorable, we learn that in the Septuagint, the ancient Greek translation of the Hebrew Bible, the passage from Jeremiah reads: "The heart is deep above all else, and so is man [sic] . . . and who shall understand him [sic]?" And in the Peshitta, the primary text used in Syriac churches, the passage says: "The heart is stronger than any man (all men) [sic]; who can understand it?" Jeremiah is not saying the human heart is deceitful. Instead, a more accurate translation says that the heart is deep and strong, and ultimately unknowable, except by God.

Wise One, help us to put aside our fear of scarcity to see the abundance of love, more than half full and running over. Make us wise so we will always choose life. May we always choose love.

REFLECTION

1. This exercise is not about whether or not we are *always* selfless, generous, or kind. It is about recognizing that we have instincts for goodness. Identify the people who depend on you, those you care for and about and any others to whom you have been kind this past week. Write down the ways you touched others. As you make a list of these instances, observe how it feels to do this exercise. Notice if you silence or diminish yourself.

2. So many of us are socialized to think about ourselves as the "glass half empty" even as this diminishes or trivializes our potential and our own goodness. Stand in front of a mirror, put your hand on your heart, and watch your reactions as you repeat these phrases aloud:

   I have the potential for goodness and my glass is half full.
   When I follow my heart instead of my ego, then my glass is half full.
   When I love my body and accept my sexuality, then my glass is half full.
   When I am kind to myself and others, then my glass is half full.
   My life is sometimes half full and sometimes it is running over.

3. Put on a pair of sunglasses or go to a store and try on sunglasses with lenses of different colors. Observe the way in which your perception of the world changes based on the lens. While wearing a pair of sunglasses, ask yourself, "What kind of stories am I telling myself about my nature that make me feel bad about myself? My body? My sexuality?" After you have identified some of these negative messages, close your eyes.

Count to ten. Remove your sunglasses and see the reality anew. Make a similar shift in your thinking with a resolution. It begins, "From this day on I will see things differently by . . ."

The Cost of Body Shame

MEDITATION

It is my eager expectation and hope
that I will not be put to shame in any way.

Philippians 1:20

What voices take up residence inside our brains? What toxic messages do we hear telling us our bodies' looks are unsatisfactory and that it is our own fault? When someone looks at another human body and arrogantly makes shame-filled judgments as to that person's value, do we listen and believe them? When we hear body shaming, or fat shaming, from social media, classmates, and even family and friends, we can easily begin to hear it internally as well. Five to ten million people in the United States, or one in fifty, suffer from what is called Body Dysmorphic Disorder, a mental health condition in which we can't stop thinking about our (perceived) defects or flaws in appearance, however small and insignificant.

There is nothing redeeming about the experience of feeling the shame that we are not good enough or not acceptable. No one is ever positively changed or liberated by shame. Nowhere is this more apparent than with adolescent girls and young adults—particularly women—who have been shamed and believe their worth and beauty are related to the numbers on a scale or limited to a particular body type. In reality, shame is a common tool of a death-dealing culture to make a profit—"buy my product and you will feel/look better"—or to change, punish, or control—"you should be ashamed of yourself for having dessert." It is also used by some churches, either by insinuation or by actually teaching the falsehood that being thin and able-bodied represents godliness while being overweight reflects a lack of willpower or a moral deficiency.

We accept these lies as reality without recognizing their absurdity. Body size, shape, or abilities never measure beauty or worth in the eyes of our Creator. In the eyes of a $75 billion weight loss industry,[7] yes, but not in the Creator's.

The priority of the apostle Paul was to live boldly in such a way that *in his* body people could see his Christ. He wrote, "It is my eager expectation and hope that I will not be put to shame in any way but that by my speaking with all boldness Christ will be exalted now as always in my body." We can eagerly expect and hope, with Paul, to live by faith and live love, speak love, and be love in our bodies. The size, shape, color, age, or ability of these bodies is simply beside the point. Shame has no place in our spiritual life. The Creator has pronounced each one of us as worthy of love and each one as "very good." All the rest is a lie.

Shameless One, too often we cower before you in fear of judgment, yet you laugh at such nonsense. We are grateful your expansive love covers us and grateful that these bodies are instruments for your love. May we be boldly confident to shamelessly proclaim that Love is the way.

REFLECTION

1. Because the presence of shame creates an empty hole inside us, we all need to have an affirmation prepared for those moments when we are tempted to feel shame. Identify one sentence that

makes you feel worthwhile and good about being who you are in your body; a statement that helps to cast out shame and build your bold confidence. Think about what it would have meant had someone close to you regularly made such a statement to you. Say it aloud and see how it feels to hear it when you add your name to it. Revise it, add to it, and correct it so that it feels exactly like what you need to hear. Keep it short enough to memorize and say it aloud often. Set an alarm and speak it aloud to yourself regularly at thirty-minute intervals for several days until it feels at home in your body.

2. Imagine God, however you envision that divinity, whispering your new affirmation before you go to sleep each night and upon awakening.
3. Shame is an ugly, smelly coat that has been wrapped around your body. When you feel ashamed, envision yourself removing this coat from your body and discard it in the nearest waste can. Repeat your affirmation.

The Perfection of Mature Wholeness

MEDITATION

Be perfect, therefore, as your heavenly Father is perfect.

Matthew 5:48

Unfortunately, when Christians are taught to seek some kind of "perfection" due to the prevalent English translation of this passage, it gets coupled with the Greco-Roman influence that believed the body/flesh inferior to the spirit. This makes sexual needs and desires dangerous and pleasure suspect. Thus, "perfection" in this verse can be conflated with "sexually pure."

At first glance, the verse seems to suggest that Jesus (uncharacteristically) commends "perfection" for his followers who, it should be remembered, bickered, sought favored status, jockeyed for seats at God's right hand, shushed the children, attempted to silence the noise of the needy, pushed away those who were too close, and either cowardly took flight or denied Jesus when the going got rough. Instead, Jesus had no such fantasy vision for his followers, nor did he teach it. Yet, our tangled understanding of "perfection" has resulted in teachings that we should be asexual, celibate, or, in the case of women particularly, virginal rather than simply being sexual people. This is the result of a misunderstanding, or, rather, a mistranslation, of the Greek word *teleios* in English as "perfect" in Matthew 5:48. The word actually means the state of a mature wholeness or completeness. The Amplified Bible, whose express purpose is to translate the fuller meanings of the original Greek words, inserts the correct meaning: "You, therefore, will be perfect [growing into spiritual maturity both in mind and character, actively integrating godly values into your daily life], as your heavenly Father is perfect." A contemporary translation in The Message captures the spiritual growth and maturity idea this way: "In a word, what I'm saying is, grow up. You're kingdom subjects. Now live like it. Live out your God-created identity. Live generously and graciously toward others, the way God lives toward you."

There are biblical passages about having pure hearts (Matthew 5:8, 1 Timothy 1:5, 2 Timothy 2:22) and having a pure mind via our thoughts (Philippians 4:8). Purity should not be conflated with perfection; rather, it is more akin to righteousness. But it is key to note that the gospel never links perfection or purity to our sexual bodies.

Jesus never expected his followers to be perfect as angels—only righteous as humans.

All That is Whole and Complete, we are humbled to consider that we are your reflection and created in the image of Complete Unity. In the face of this, we are painfully aware of our shortcomings and failures. Remind us to celebrate with gratitude and in humility that you are not finished with us yet. Make us complete as we mature to become who you envision us to be.

REFLECTION

1. A thought experiment: We can only intuit the complete and utter wholeness of All That Is whom we name as God. But what would the wholeness of spiritual maturity for humanity look like? How would we live together as a global family? What decisions would we make about resolving conflict? Sharing resources? What festivals would we plan? What would be the rules (if any) about our bodies? Sexuality?
2. Describe yourself, your life, your behavior, your choices if you could miraculously attain the status of being as fully mature and completely human as God is fully mature and complete as divine. What would you do differently? What beliefs about yourself need to be challenged? What choices would you make differently?
3. Make one resolution today of what you can do to shift your thinking away from powerlessness and immobility because of perfectionistic standards and toward more spiritual maturity and completeness.

Covering our Shame

MEDITATION

*God made garments of skins for the man
and for his wife, and clothed them.*

Genesis 3:21

According to the Hebrew Bible story of the Garden of Eden, it was having the choice to become knowledgeable about good and evil that tested and ultimately created a sense of shame for the first couple. Their instinct after eating the fruit from the tree and having their eyes opened was to cover their nakedness.

It is worth noting that as long as they were with the Creator, no garments had been necessary because no shame was present. When one is surrounded by Love and lives in Love, then the knowledge of good and evil is unnecessary. Why? Because when we are engulfed in Loving Presence there is no evil, only goodness. Love's protection is all the covering we need.

Body coverings can be used as a tease about sexuality but they also hide vulnerability. Covering our bodies to hide our sexuality as if we were not sexual beings can protect us from unwanted stares, intrusive gestures, and, we hope, from harm itself. Some arguments posit that coverings prevent distractions although there is evidence that attempts to cover and hide our bodies create a greater, hidden, enticement. Whatever the motives as the first earth creatures covered their shame, the Creator's understanding response was compassionately to make the garments they would need as they began their journey into the world.

Now, as we live outside the Garden, good and evil are well known. Yet the garments compassionately provided still linger. Unconditional love. Undeserved forgiveness. Unexpected grace. When and where good and evil are present, this protection continues. There is no need for shame. The love of the Creator covers our vulnerability.

One Who Understands, thank you for understanding our nakedness and fears of exposure. Keep reminding us that whether inside the Garden or out, whether we know good from evil or not, your love is an abiding presence always near to us. Remove our shame for being human but especially remove our shame at being sexual humans.

REFLECTION

1. Thought Experiment: (Read the following slowly and have a blanket on hand.) Most of us have some regret regarding decisions we have made about our body or sexual behaviors, so envision yourself in this Garden hiding with the first two earth creatures. In hindsight, we become aware of our poor choices and feel shame. Imagine hiding, fearful that you will be punished. You shiver in the cold. Yet, while there are consequences for our decisions and actions, you discover that a loving Creator is concerned about your well-being and hands you a warm garment. (Wrap yourself in the blanket.) Imagine putting on this garment that was sized to fit your body. As you feel the fabric, feel the compassion of the One who is with you. Let the chill of fear leave your body as compassion covers you. Imagine the Creator whispering these words,

"Do not be afraid.
I will never abandon or forsake you.
Do not be afraid."

2. Experiential activity: Sometimes we carry our shame like a bag. Rather than holding onto the things that get in our way, as shame inevitably does, and rather than drag these bags of pain and shame, we must let it go. Why? Because when we love ourselves and let Love move through our bodies we begin to heal. What bag of shame are you carrying that you need to jettison? To release any shameful burden that is in your bag, write it out on a piece of paper and then burn it or discard it. Remove it from your mind and, should it return, remind yourself to let it go. In Christian language, give it to God and leave it there. Let it go. It does not require constant petitions or begging for continual forgiveness. God always forgives. It is over, so let it go.
3. Take a deep breath and slowly read aloud each of these affirmations:

   "I am worthwhile." (Repeat)
   "I am beautiful and amazing. "(Repeat)
   "I have sexual rights and freedoms." (Repeat)
   "I am not other people's stereotypes." (Repeat)
   "I am part of a wider family." (Repeat)

Standing in Our Courage

MEDITATION

Most blessed of women be Yael.[8]

Judges 5:24

One of the sheroes in the Hebrew scripture is Yael who, upon being confronted by Sisera, the cowardly commander who had abandoned his defeated regiment, used the opportunity to drive a tent peg through his skull while he was sleeping. Perhaps she had reached her limit of the carnage from men's wars and acted on her instincts to stop one of the key instigators. Her courageous act required planning, guile, and intelligence.

While Yael's murderous response was extreme, do we keep our eyes open for times when we must intervene and say, "Enough is enough"? Do we step in when we hear people berating children? Acting out of racial bigotry? Causing harm by bashing gays or mistreating gender variant people? Do we intervene when females are treated as sex objects or speak out when someone is being shamed or bullied? Or, do we say, "That is awful but it is none of my business."

Yael took things into her own hands. She had a plan and a tent peg. What tools do we have on hand to protect the most vulnerable bodies in our midst? It certainly does not require tent pegs to stand up to hypocrites, sexual bullies, or loud-mouthed "pleasure police." Rather, it requires the courage and willingness to speak up and speak out on behalf of those being threatened and even to advocate for ourselves. Courage and the willingness to name body injustice and sexual harm are the weapons we need to advocate and protect the "least of these" as Jesus commanded (Matthew 25:40, 45).

Hateful words, gossip, stereotypes, and the use of fear to control others all harm us and ultimately diminish our humanity. When harmful behavior is in evidence, we must have courage and take heart. After Yael rises up and says, "No more!" her story ends with these words: all of the "land had rest forty years" (3:11).*

Strong Courageous One, we confess we often fear standing up for what is right, especially if it creates conflict or thrusts us into the spotlight. Help us to lean into your strength and rely on your goodness. Righteous living is always courageous living so prepare us to intervene on behalf of all your children.

REFLECTION

1. The gospel story reveals that Jesus was aware that the residents of Jerusalem were fickle and in need of his presence even as the city was dangerously filled with his enemies. Yet he courageously entered the city to intervene on their behalf. Can you name a time when you pushed through your fear and took a courageous stand? If not, what held you back? If so, was it the right thing to do?
2. Name the groups of people around you who might be judged, criticized, or harmed because of their sexuality or their bodies. Now name people you know personally or have heard of in the media who have been publicly shamed or harmed for their sexuality or their bodies. Put yourself in their position: what would you want or need from others to get through this difficult time? What intervention is needed?

---

*For a contrasting meditation on the importance of not intervening see "The Unhelpful Helping Hand."

3. In South Africa there has been a national campaign to keep alive the inspiring memory of Nelson Mandela and his commitment to social justice in his country. It is captured in the phrase used to encourage people, "Be a Nelson." We could guess that in Israel after Yael's story became widely known some might have said, "Be a Yael." Identify four courageous people you admire. Now move your body into a posture that reflects that sense of courage and strength. As you are in that posture, call to mind those four people and complete these sentences with their name as you address yourself.

"(Your name), be a (their name)"
"(Your name), be a (their name)"
"(Your name), be a (their name)"
"(Your name), be a (their name)"

Subverting Order with Play

MEDITATION

We played the flute for you and you did not dance.

Matthew 11:17

Jesus noted that dour religious professionals could not hear the music, nor could they dance. And yet, still today, play is seldom part of our religious life. In fact, sometimes the level of religiosity is demonstrated by the severity of the grim faces. Why is this so?

The problem with patriarchy is not only that it favors men and rewards toxic masculinity—although it does—but that it assumes a hierarchy: that men are at the top and others must always be at the bottom. The religious idea supporting this arrangement is often framed as a "natural order." Unfortunately, this gets implemented as a hierarchical spiritual ranking as well: Father God is on top, followed by men, supposedly because of their resemblance to Father God.[9] They are followed by women, particularly white, heterosexual, virginal, or married women. This orderly ladder has at the very bottom rung non-binary, gender fluid or trans, gay, poor people, and people of color, but especially non-first-world, Indigenous, immigrant, or refugee bodies.

Note that it is not possible within this framework to be playful and keep order at the same time. Play, by definition, is a joyful release, while order in the context of human bodies is about control. Order contains and hampers movement, difference, and variety. It keeps a lid on playful sexual impulses, choosing rules over delight.

The Creator is obviously not orderly. Compared to the wild diversity of creation, order is simply ridiculous. In fact, while keeping order prevents play, play itself explores, challenges, and often upsets order just to see what happens! Play is curious and unpredictable. It is about doing the unexpected and taking delight in surprises. Play is most important in our sexual lives.

So rather than seeking a "natural order" in our faith, let's seek instead those expansive faith experiences that can move us toward joy. We may discover that the path of joy is also the path to the Sacred.

Playful Creator, the giraffe's ridiculous neck, the male sea horse's pregnancies, and the jellyfish's eerie, other-worldly floating existence reflect your playful delight in variety and surprise. Yet we cling to the comfort of order hoping for protection or reassurance. Forgive us when we refuse to dance exuberantly in joy of the gift of life. Remove our fear so we may dance.

REFLECTION

1. In describing the peaceable kingdom, Isaiah said, "a little child shall lead them." (11:6b) For, until trained otherwise, children often follow their instincts of curiosity and seek pleasure and joy in each activity of discovery. What were the rules about playing or being playful when you were a child? What were the limits? What happened if the rules for order were disobeyed?
2. Following an orderly ladder of domination only holds if we all agree. Is there a story in Jesus's life or teaching that supports separating people into orderly categories that might privilege certain bodies over others?
3. Make a list of biblical characters or Jesus stories when people did the unexpected and surprising thing. (Hint: it was usually at God's command.)
4. If Jesus is playing the flute and asking you to dance in your life, how would you dance today? What would give you joy even if, or maybe because, it violates the orderly expectations? Is joy worth taking a risk?
5. Put on some music with a rhythm that calls you to dance and move your body!
6. Go to a mirror and make the oddest, silliest, most fun face that you possibly can. Do it again and make a crazier one. After you are satisfied with the wildest one, if you dare, show it to someone else. And when they ask what you are doing, tell them it's a warmup of your spiritual exercise to subvert order with play.

Self-Confident Authenticity

MEDITATION

If I proclaim the gospel, this gives me no grounding for boasting.

1 Corinthians 9:16

The chief job of our ego is to keep us safe. But, in performing this task, the ego will often play it safe not to attract attention to itself. Yes, being seen by others is a way to reassure ourselves of our value—our egos appreciate the attention of grandstanding. Our spiritual work is to recognize when our ego is out of balance. This is especially apparent when we want recognition for our spiritual lives. Our ego says, "Look at me!" It wants to be known as a holy person and the one with the answers. When we feel deep satisfaction that we are right or we judge when others are wrong or misguided, that is ego. However, the act of removing our ego can also be egotistical. When we undercut our own value, pile on heaps of self-criticism, and feel badly for being unable to meet some spiritual standard, that is also ego! The apostle Paul argues that our egos have no business boasting. Church membership, good deeds, some forms of sexual purity, or correcting or saving people from their sexual identities and decisions is not part of the gospel in any shape or form. Rather, the gospel instructs us to have the mind of Christ (1 Corinthians 2:16), which means to live into our authentic self, the one that the ego tries to control.

The authentic Christ mind seeks a balance—we are neither gods nor the lowliest of sinners. When we move out of our egos and move into our authenticity, we begin to understand that all of this is not about us. Rather, it is all about love. When the ego's calls to "Notice me!" are removed, we begin to understand that all that matters is for the love of God to saturate our being and release in an outward flow toward others. Loved into existence, we accept and love ourselves, not as perfect beings, not as the most sexually pure Christian, but as wondrous vessels designed as containers for Love. Thus, to have the mind of Christ is to find a counterbalance to our egos, never boasting, but living into our authentic selves with confidence.

Selfless One, forgive us when we do not acknowledge your longing to saturate us with your love. When we forget, we try to fill ourselves with the praise of others or beat our chests at our woeful inadequacy. Remind us to walk tall by loving who we are, not as ego-driven, but rather as love-centered. Center us to put on the mind of Christ with the sole task of loving. Then our eyes will open to see those places where love needs to flow. Then, as we are filled with the mind of Christ, we will have confidence that we are sufficient.

REFLECTION

1. Journal assignment:
    a. If the ego wants to keep you safe by showing the world your perfection, what are the ways you maintain a public face that shows no imperfection? What are your cover-ups of choice?
    b. What is your ego afraid of disclosing? Identify the fear your ego has about being known. "If I let people know ______ about me, then I fear ______ will happen." How likely is this fear to happen?
    c. Who are the people or the situations that feel safe to you? Who accepts you as the authentic you? And where does

the Divine fit into this? Is your God accepting and loving or harshly judgmental? Where did that image come from?

2. Thought Experiment: What would it feel like to be saturated with love? Imagine the air as God's Love waiting to enter your lungs, waiting to warm or cool your body. Wave your hands over your body as if you are pushing the air onto your entire body so it will move into your pores. Now touch your body with reassurance that it is sufficient. You are sufficient. Put your hands on your heart and say, "I am loved."

Sacred Embodiment

MEDITATION

Do you not realize that Jesus Christ is in you?

2 Corinthians 13:5

Instead of focusing on virginity, celibacy, and exclusive heterosexual monogamy, what if we acted as if we believed that we "live and move and have our being" *in* God, as Luke records Paul teaching the Atheneans (Acts 17:28)? Or, similarly, what if we believed that Jesus is *in* us as Paul taught (2 Corinthians 13:5)? Incarnation means God is *in* Jesus, and Jesus is incarnated as God-in-the-flesh, and God is *in* us as fleshly beings (Paul's teachings to Corinth) while we are *in* God (Paul's teachings to Athens). Both build on the early church's memory that Jesus taught, "I am in my Father, and you in me, and I in you" (John 14:20).

This is an encompassing circle, a replaying loop: We are in the Sacred. The Sacred is in us . . . in these bodies. But if we live in shame about fleshly bodies, sexual feelings, desires, and needs, then we miss this interconnecting union. If flesh is the embodiment of the Divine, then sexual sin cannot be reduced to physical acts of sex. Rather, sexual sin would be the failure to acknowledge fleshly existence reflects the Sacred. When we fail to recognize the sacredness of our physicality, we deny the interconnectedness of divinity within our lives. Indeed, it is precisely *because* we are in these earthly sexual bodies that spiritual insight happens. We channel the Spirit through our relating, loving, forgiving, and justice-making ways, always in and through these bodies. The fourteenth-century mystic, St. Julian of Norwich, captured this idea, "God is in our sensuality, for in the same instant and place in which our soul is made sensual . . . exists the city of God."

When we act in respectful, honest, and authentic ways, we are living, moving, and having our being in the Sacred (Acts 17:28). Then we channel the intimacy of the Spirit of Love through every bodily encounter and every physical expression of connection.

Indwelling One, you are as near as our breath and as close as our heart. When we breathe, we can feel your presence. When we are still, we can lay aside a rushed and hurried life and our public self and remember you are always here with us, in us, for us, calling to us. "Be still" you say. "Be real" you admonish. "Breathe." And we give thanks.

REFLECTION

1. Guided Meditation: The River of Forgiveness

   Many of us have an ongoing recording in our head that shames or criticizes us for bad choices or past actions. If this is true for you, imagine the following:

   You are going to take a swim in a lovely, slow-moving river near a quiet, peaceful place of beauty where you are not afraid.

If you cannot swim, the water is knee deep. If you don't like fish, there are none. If you don't like mud, wear special shoes. Now, as you imagine undressing, you see pieces of paper stuck to your entire body, each with a negative message about your body, your past, or messes you have made. They cover you like feathers of negativity. Imagine stepping into the clear, peaceful serenity of water and slowly moving away from the shore. You are safe. The water temperature is warm. Slowly move your body, swaying gently side to side. And as you move, realize the tiny bits of paper cannot survive this imaginary river but dissolve. Run your hands over your body to loosen those messages. Rub your arms. Brush your abdomen and legs. If the messages are close to your heart, then rub and pat your heart to let them go. If related to your sexuality, then gently caress your own genital area. Let the negative messages dissolve into the River of Forgiveness. When you emerge, the messages are gone. Should you notice later that you hear more negative messages, return and go "down by the riverside." Return to bathe in the waters of Love.

2. Compassion is sacred. Identify a time you said or did a kindness to another person as a gift that might have been unexpected. Now add a second instance. Think about what each experience felt like. Watch how your heart swells as you remember how good it feels to be compassionate toward someone else. That swelling is acknowledging the sacred.

When the Body is Compromised

MEDITATION

Consider my affliction and my trouble...

Psalm 25:18

Just because we are made in the image of God and the Creator pronounced all creation as very good does not mean we are somehow divinely protected from life's ups and downs. Our choice is to make the most of whatever life hands us. Nowhere is this more evident and more challenging than when our bodies age or are ill.

While all bodies will eventually do so, this profound reality is incredibly difficult for us to accept. Yet the autoimmune system breaks down and we are left with chronic pain; a diagnosis is given that may prove fatal; a fall, stroke, or accident unexpectedly occurs; congenital issues impact the ability to walk, hear, see, or live unencumbered even as an uninterrupted eight-hour sleep becomes a fantasy and productive work becomes impossible. An ableist society prefers the illusion these events won't or don't happen. Thus, we blame or shame or ignore. The message is clear: to have a body that is not "healthy" by the standards of society is to live a deficient life.

People who live with chronic ailments, some named and treatable and some not, are some of the most resilient problem solvers. A requirement for survival with a compromised body involves learning to adapt and to be in each moment with its gasps, pains, and ongoing limits. It is to be deeply attentive to the body's needs and, with strength and resilience, cling to the sacred promise that, however compromised, all bodies are wondrously created. Disability justice then requires that we find or help create supportive communities that understand, sometimes firsthand, the obstacles faced and, when there is energy, to call out an insensitive and oblivious ableist society for having a compassion deficit.

The gospels indicate Jesus cared a lot about bodies that were compromised, and yet he did not heal all the lepers, the blind, or the lame in Palestine. Some remained unhealed. The good news is that a full life of responsibility, wisdom, maturity, joy, and a wide community of caring friendships is possible regardless of the state of our bodies.

One who stands in the gaps, thank you for your presence in every struggle. Remind us that your Love reaches through every oxygen tent, arrives in every cup of herbal tea and every medication that, at least for a time, gets us through. You are in every person who touches, lifts, wipes, and caresses our bodies and in every creative solution that makes life possible or better. We are grateful for every person whose life exudes patience in the midst of pain, who accept even as they defy their circumstance, whose courage and strength reveal that friendship and survival are gifts that show we are all more than our bodies. Remind us that while some bodies require more upkeep, they are always our holy temple.

REFLECTION

1. Experiential Activity: Sit or lie quietly in a comfortable position and try to block all distractions while you listen to and respond to your body. What is it saying? Are you comfortable? Tense? Aching? Anxious? Once you have adjusted and settled into silence, move into a deeper level of listening. Pay attention to the hum of your body by noting the rhythmic

sounds of your breathing and the beating of your heart. Feel yourself at home in a machine whose only function is to care for you. Sometimes it does so imperfectly and yet, it continues doing so. Offer a prayer of gratitude.

2. Make a list of the people you know who live with compromised bodies. Note those you have contacted in the last week or to whom you have recently offered your assistance. Indicate the name(s) of individuals you can reach out to today. Remember, it is not about giving pity. You are not their savior. Rather, it is about seeing each person as whole and acknowledging their unique life challenges.

The Unhelpful Helping Hand

MEDITATION

Why do you see the speck in your neighbor's eye . . . ?

Matthew 7:3

A small cactus sits near my writing desk. Its leaves are tough and thick and filled with the liquid that it needs to survive during long months in the desert. Though its native habitat looks parched, I am tempted to water it. If I yield to this impulse, it will die. It doesn't need my help. The wisdom is inside itself, listening to its own needs and adjusting accordingly. How much damage do we do when we appoint ourselves as "helpers" because we think we know what is right for others? Our motivation might be to improve their situation or encourage a course correction based on what would be the wrong choice for us. Yet, regardless of our intentions, this improvement strategy is simply interference, or worse yet, such "help" may be to the other's detriment. It is important to recognize that we are far more likely to judge others if we have felt judged ourselves—either by others or by our internal critics. We project that sense of judgment rather than working with it in ourselves. After all, how could we possibly know what others need or who they should love and how they should express that love? Others' lives are not ours to judge.

We are all prone to engage in this classic situation of imposing "help." Sometimes this justifies our own choices. Other times it is to correct someone we think is headed in the wrong direction and sometimes we think God wants us to do so. Unfortunately, playing God can be justified by telling ourselves this is helping. And so we just keep pouring in more of what we think is right while our moralistic judgments slowly drown the roots of whatever love we might hope to express.*

Sufficient One, forgive us when we arrogantly think we know what is best for others when their experiences are not ours. We may want to help yet, if we are honest, sometimes we want them to change because it makes us more comfortable. Remind us that you are their help so we will silence unasked-for advice. Teach us not to impose our agendas or expectations on others but to channel your Love through our own lives. You are sufficient. Forgive us when we forget.

REFLECTION

1. Activity: Every issue involving helping others has a related issue of the need for consent. Usually we help (interfere) without asking first. When we believe that the state of other

*For a contrasting meditation on the importance of intervention see "Standing in Our Courage."

people's souls is our responsibility, we can be guilty of moving into people's lives without consent. (Perhaps they do not want to be saved by our religion!)

If asking for what you want or if hearing rejection is difficult for you, ask a friend to do this exercise with you. Their only job is to say "no" every time. Think of a series of invitations to a wide variety of fun or exciting things they would like to do or offer to help them in important ways. Keep asking as they respond negatively each time. Play for three minutes and then talk about what it felt like repeatedly to be told no. Your friend can talk about what it felt like to keep pushing back on your great suggestions. Then, reverse roles to experience refusing to give consent.[10]

2. Who in your life has tried to be helpful when you didn't appreciate it? Did you tell them? If not, why not? How did this impact your relationship? If this situation feels unfinished, write a letter to this person describing what they did and how you felt about it. Do not send it. This is your spiritual work to do, not theirs. Remember this experience when you have the urge to offer unasked for advice or suggestions that you think will be helpful. After all, sometimes would-be helpers are not helpers at all.

Where are You?

MEDITATION

Where are you?

Genesis 3:9

After experiencing deep trauma, a long-time vocalist discovered that she could no longer sing. Singing required too much vulnerability and she simply could not reveal herself. As a result, without music it seemed the color was gone from her life. Shades of gray were all that remained. One day her vocal teacher suggested she write a letter to her now silent and colorless voice and, as she did, to her surprise, she saw a vision of swirling colors emerging from a whirlwind and heard a voice say:

> Take courage
> Descend to the depths of your roots
> Roots that coil toward an authentic center
> Centering-still and steady
> Steadily expanding into blushes of color
> Colorful palettes tinged with blushing
> Blushes of complex hues
> Hues of authenticity
> Authentic energy
> Energetically bursting into freedom
> Freely singing
> Far outside the lines
> Wild colors escaping

Far beyond the lines
Take courage
Look and follow.[11]

The vision of swirling colors she now saw were still churning inside her waiting to escape into musical forms with tornado-like power. Soon the music returned to her life. So often, pain or personal struggles make us fearfully vulnerable, so that, like the first earth creatures who hid in the Garden of Eden, we too hide and cover the nakedness of our deepest desires and longings. But even as we may cower in fear, uncertainty, or pain, sometimes covered in guilt and shame, Love in all its vibrant colors comes to make us whole. This Wisdom calls to us, "Where are you?" Then, like the vocalist who found her voice, in the gray corners of our vulnerable hiding places, we too may discover that we are already fully known and extravagantly loved. The colors of our true self are coiled in our authentic voice waiting to escape into the music of our lives. This Love encourages us to go deep inside to let our roots down into the soil of our authenticity—not toward perfection, but toward our authentic center where the Sacred awaits. From this center we can explode into all the untamed colors that we are made to display. Then we can fully respond to the invitation of Life. Birthing wild exuberant colors, we come into our own. Blossoming into brilliance we sing, "Here I am."

O Love that will not let us go, you want us to sing our life's song with all the wild colors of our authentic selves yet we often prefer to remain hidden. Thank you for coming to find us when we try to hide our true selves that you made us to be. Give us courage to believe you can love us into wholeness and may we confidently reveal the colors hiding inside. May we sing our own song wildly and freely.

REFLECTION

1. Because of the many taboos about sexuality, we often hide, pretending we aren't sexual or wearing the masks of who we think others want us to be. In our hiding, oftentimes we crouch in shame and fear of judgment. Make a list of the times you hide that begins, "I am hiding when I…"

2. After your list has been compiled, ask, "Where are you?" then read the first one aloud by saying, "I am hiding when I…" Then respond with, "You are one of a kind. Do not be afraid." Repeat with each of the items on your list.

   (Question) "Where are you?"
   (Answer) "I am hiding when I…"
   (Response) "You are one of a kind. Do not be afraid."

3. Experiential Activity: What colors depict your state of mind and your life? Draw an abstract picture of yourself with the focus not on your likeness but on the colors that you chose. Then draw a color of the music that emerges from your throat as you speak your truth, tell your story, state your boundaries, and ask for what you want. What colors emerge?

part two

Sexual Bodies as Sacred?

Think On these Things

The mouths of the righteous utter wisdom,
and their tongues speak justice.

Psalm 37:30

While there is much glorification of sex in US culture through the media, fashion, advertising, and other outlets, we are, for the most part, sexually confused and uninformed and thus sexually wounded. We do not, as a rule, understand the breadth of sexual diversity in humans or in the natural world. We lack cross-cultural exposure and knowledge, and have little understanding of the sexual misogyny, bias, blinders and blunders of those (both historically and in the present day) who interpreted and wrote Christian dogma that split body from spirit. It is no wonder, then, that confusion and ignorance combine to create wounding. As a result, ill-informed sexual decisions are made, mistakes occur, and abuse can result. A sexually repressive theology that results from splitting the body from the spirit is one that focuses primarily on physical body parts as problematic to spirituality. It does not see that hearts and the spirit are intricately intertwined with the body so that mind, body, and spirit are all avenues to the Divine. Such a disconnected theology contributes to this ignorance by the creation of rules and beliefs that are harmful. Rigid gender rules and roles in our society can contribute to the injustice of violated boundaries and a lack of informed consent. These violations are, at their core, unhealthy sexual behaviors that can create emotional and physical wounds and long-lasting guilt.

This guilt and woundedness can then become an internalized shame that confirms our own lack of worth and value. Both guilt and shame can manifest as sexual dysfunction and influence our ability to experience intimacy or engage in a healthy manner in intimate relationships. Many of us, but particularly those exposed to a large dose of body-negative religion, experience fear of our sexual bodies, the bodies of others, and particularly those bodies that we perceive as different from our own. This fear not only harms our ability to be in relationship, whether with ourselves or others, but it also distorts our self-esteem and sexual self-confidence. The constant obsession in the culture about certain body types, build, and abilities, shapes, sizes, and color can become a disrespect of most bodies. This toxic combination of guilt, shame, fear, disrespect, and the rules and expectations we may learn both from the culture and from our faith community can leave us deeply conflicted, even as we live in a pluralistic culture of many different body shapes and sizes. Result? We all have issues with the body, so welcome to the club.

The focus in the following section is to help dismantle some of these harmful ideas and to identify how we hold this negativity in our minds and memory but also inside our bodies. It is a call to heal ourselves and one another and to see beloved humanity through the benevolent eyes of the Divine.

As we "utter wisdom" and "speak justice" (Psalm 37:30), we will refuse to accept that guilt and shame or fear are good. Instead, it is right and just to name the deficiencies of those cultural and religious rules that diminish our bodies as objects to be controlled, used, abused, exploited, denied and discarded, or stereotyped and diminished. Further, it is unjust to push the human body into submission to rules and roles that do not fit or are not freely chosen. To be spiritually wise and "utter wisdom" is to challenge the cultural and religious limitations on joy and delight when those actions are ethical and consensual. In our wisdom, we contradict body negativity with acceptance, forgiveness, and affirmation that flow in a stream of grace-filled Love directly from the Divine. Wisdom acknowledges a beautifully sensual humanity freely existing with possibility and potential for generosity and kindness; enjoying every minute in full companionship and intimate relatedness in our lives. This vision begins by meditating upon our own bodies. For it is how we love our own bodies that determines how well we will be able to love the bodies of others (Matthew 22:39).

Think on these things as you consider the following meditations on your pleasurable, beautiful sensual body:

- How much do you love yourself and your body?
- How do you experience the sacred through your bodily experiences and sensations?
- What does beauty on the inside and the outside look like?
- When do you feel the most beautiful?
- How much courage does it take to be wise and call for justice for all bodies?

The Silence and the Senses

MEDITATION

Be still, and know that I am…

Psalm 46:10

Needing a retreat into silence and solitude, I cleared the calendar and made plans: no interruptions, no distractions, nobody around but me. It would be wonderful. But once settled into retreat mode and waiting for a refill to my creative well, I began to realize that I was not alone. Every day a small gecko scurried around my patio. This tiny lizard was only about four inches long but full of energy. And, though timid, it was neither interested nor threatened by my presence. Apparently, it too needed solitude and silence. As I sat in the afternoon sunshine on another rather quiet day, I realized that there was also a yellow butterfly, or perhaps a moth, that regularly joined me in the garden. Fluttering, sniffing, sampling, it flew away only to return to its interruption of my solitude. In the evening, I discovered that the crows gathered in the nearby trees to hold a town hall meeting, no doubt summarizing the day's exploits and announcing the coming attractions for tomorrow. Oblivious to this interruption for others and paying no attention to me, they squawked and chattered to one another at day's end.

In my supposed silence there were so many creatures leading their own busy lives: geckos, crows, and butterflies. It was soon apparent that the more I quieted my brain, the more my senses opened to nature's sights and sounds. It's possible that the more we try to remove ourselves from a busy world, the more we see how connected we are. But if we do not slow down, we will miss it all: the town hall chatter of the crows, the fluttering beauty of fragile wings, the scurrying steps of a gecko. Or perhaps we miss the still, small whispers of the Divine in our ears.

Creator God, thank you for the small wonders in our natural world, especially those smallest of creatures who lend to the world their unique beauty. Forgive us when we get lost in busyness, unable to see or take in the intricate miracles of life happening all around us. Turn off the distractions in our brains, for only then will we open our eyes to your sensual world.

REFLECTION

1. When is it easier to turn off distractions and when can you more easily listen and observe the natural world? Where are the places that are conducive to such listening? What changes do you need to make to create more opportunities to listen and be still?
2. Sometimes we keep ourselves busy and distracted because we do not want to hear a truth that we are repressing or simply don't want to address. Perhaps it is about ourselves, the choices we have made, or a specific unhappiness or discomfort with our lives. Listening without avoiding can feel uncomfortable and difficult. The psalmist reassures us that in the stillness we can feel an abiding Presence with us, by our side. Ask yourself if there is a specific reason you avoid making the time to be still and listen. Set aside a designated time for a Silent Retreat when you will neither hear other people nor speak aloud yourself. Take note of your comfort level in complete, extended silence.

3. Experiential activity: Assume a comfortable seated position and vow to listen for fifteen minutes. Begin by saying the following, taking three breaths between each line.

   Be still and know that I am God. (Breathe)
   Be still and know that I am (Breathe)
   Be still and know (Breathe)
   Be still (Breathe)
   Be (Breathe)*

Olives, Grapes, and Sex

MEDITATION

A good land, a land with flowing streams,
with springs and underground waters welling up
in valleys and hills, a land of wheat and barley,
of vines and fig trees and pomegranates,
a land of olive trees and honey.

Deuteronomy 8:7,8

Since vineyards did not exist in my Midwestern world, I thought a grape was a grape, either green or red, and olives were either black or, appropriately, olive green. I have since learned there is a difference in the taste, color, or shapes of olives depending on where they were grown and in grapes depending on the varietal and terroir. In fact, there are over 10,000 types of grapes and there are twenty types of olives, although they're not distinguished based on

*To further explore this exercise, go to the reflection on "Reconnecting the Body and Spirit."

color. All this diversity is not as amazing as was the superficial understanding that I thought of as truth; my world was just too small. How often we assume we have grasped truth when in reality we have failed to see nuance and variation. The more we delve into any topic, the more complex it becomes. The problem, of course, is that since we don't know what we don't know, we can easily conclude that we know it all!

This is true when it comes to sexual tastes and interests. Just as I may have been tempted to turn away from an unfamiliar grape or an olive, if I prejudge and reflexively turn away from a sexual experience that is new or unexpected, I may miss out on a sensual or sexual delight. Rather than settling for the familiarity of a consistent diet, we could enjoy an exquisite feast of the senses that originated from the Creator. By remaining curious and open to new experiences, we enrich our life.

Creator beyond categories, thank you for the times and ways you surprise us with difference, nuance, and complexity. Forgive us when we settle into familiar patterns and, in our comfort, assume this is all there is to enjoy in the life you give. We confess that such an attitude tempts us to conclude ours is the true experience. Keep us curious about your wide-ranging world. Give us courage to be open to new ideas and experiences that can enhance our lives, expand our horizons, and, deepen our joy and satisfaction with your amazing world.

REFLECTION

1. Identify something in nature that intrigues you but which you have never given much thought to exploring. Search the internet or in your local library and learn more about this topic. Then reread the prayer to the Creator beyond categories.

2. As we seek to remove any guilt or shame which constrain us, opening ourselves to more sexual freedom, we will need to understand our private and deepest fantasies and desires. While this can feel scary, it can also introduce us to more nuanced and varied experiences of our sexuality. This deeper exploration, when guilt and shame are absent, can, if we choose, broaden our understanding of ourselves. Take some time to identify any fears of exploring your primal passions. Where do they come from? Then ask, can you accept that the Creator made humanity diverse with a wide imagination for pleasure? Why or why not?
3. Individuals can enjoy a wide variety of sexual behaviors. If this interests you, watch my YouTube series "Sex is Good."

Losing Ourselves in Creation

MEDITATION

For I am about to create…

Isaiah 65:17

As an amateur mosaic artist, I know the delight in creating something without knowing what the project will look like when finished. Instead, in letting go of preconceived ideas, it is possible to approach the mosaic tiles and simply watch what happens when the imagination takes over. The sole criterion is to find joy in the process of creation and to delight in the artwork that emerges.

But creating requires silencing our Inner Critic and Judge, both of whom will say, "This will not be any good!" By releasing our inner critic and ego and being open to creatively play, we may find the great thrill of discovery of our imaginations. Suddenly, the inner artist that resides in all of us can see possibilities that were not planned. What a lesson to consider. What would happen if we lived in the freedom of having no expectations? If, by silencing our Inner Critic and Judge, we could free ourselves from our own judgment and the sting of criticism? Wouldn't we have more fun? Wouldn't we enjoy our lives in playful ways and, perhaps, in more creative ways as well? Is it possible that the Creator is waiting for us to get out of our own way so that wonderful and surprising things can begin to happen in our lives? Perhaps the spiritual call is to take a chance on the Divine and let go to see what will happen. Just a thought . . .

Creative Artist, you set us free to live abundant lives in the freedom of love. Free us from the notion that we are or should be in control so that we can let you guide the artistry of our lives. Set us free to be open to life with all its possibilities. Astonish us with new insights and new understandings. Be the Artist of our lives, knocking us off our feet in praise and gratitude. And then, may we fall on our knees in humility, knowing we are blessed.

REFLECTION

1. Today be creative, but not with the expectation of making a professional finished project of some kind. In fact, don't plan to show it to anyone. Rather, the goal is to make or do something creative that will be fun, whether it be a creative moment, a creative conversation, a creative project, or taking the next step on a creative idea.
2. If you managed to do this, journal about how it felt to play and enjoy the creative moment. If this is outside your comfort

level, have a conversation with the Creator in your journal. Write with your dominant hand why this is difficult and then, with your non-dominant hand, write the answer that emerges as the Creator Artist's response.

3. Imagine a Creator fashioning the human body from the particles of dust in the earth. What part of the human body do you think would give a Playful Creator the most delight to create? Sit with the image of a chuckling Creator until it makes you chuckle as well.

Sensory Invitation

MEDITATION

Look, a little cloud no bigger than a person's hand
is rising out of the sea.

1 Kings 18:44

Imagine the following sensual scenario as if you were sitting on a park bench near a downtown park.

First, you see a middle-aged male body slowly push itself along the sidewalk with one leg while the other rests horizontally on a scooter. Another human body is following a playful dog who is exhilarated to be off leash. A little body about four years old runs past as quickly as those short little brown legs can run, maybe chasing butterflies or the dog, maybe just for the sheer joy of moving! Next is a passing family group of slightly overweight bodies deep in conversation as their children playfully walk or skip alongside. The well-behaved children are absorbed in the freedom of the warm spring day, oblivious to the adults. Now you see that there are more bodies coming up the sidewalk, each moving at different speeds through this dimension we call space. Right now, here, in this time and space, each can detect a whiff of cinnamon and sugar coming from a corner bakery. It mingles with the smell of the sea air. The sound from the next block over is of surf crashing onto shore. A snapshot moment, even in imagination. Indeed, each moment is, never to be experienced again.

This is a sensory invitation in a spiritual life. It is a call to stop and take it all in. Take it in. Every last drop. Become watchful, hear the insistent call, the stream of sensual inputs. In our self-importance it is easy to shut it all out, yet these sights and sounds and smells inform, enrich, and enliven our spirits. Can we move out of our heads and move instead into our body? What sensory delights would bless our daily lives if we paid attention? Can we do that?

Wondrous Creator, what gifts of abundance! Awaken our senses to the little things: puffs of clouds, rushing water sounds, flowers' fragrance, laughing children, cuddly kittens, warm hugs. Make us aware of the little touches of wonder available for us. Open our mind to take in the wonder of living. And, if need be, turn up the volume of the sensory alarm so we might respond with awe and thanksgiving. Our world is wonderful and awesome. Thank you.

REFLECTION

1. The more we become sensually aware, the deeper the possibilities for awe and wonder at the gift of life. With these changes, the deeper our spirits can then move into gratitude for our sensual lives in these incredible bodies. Put your senses on alert now and look up from your reading. What do

you see? Hear? Smell? What are you touching? Take it all in deeply. Take a deep breath and breathe in the wonder.

Some find moving into the senses difficult because the senses can be triggers for memories. If this happens, allow the memories and tears to surface. Be gentle with yourself. Some memories bring tears because of the joy they recall; others are more hurtful. Acknowledging painful memories and the emotions that accompany them is a step toward healing. Comfort yourself until the feelings subside. And, if it is helpful, imagine the Spirit of Love bringing comfort. It may help to get up and move about physically. Imagine every step is a movement toward healing. If painful memories continue, talk with someone you trust, whether a friend or a professional therapist.

2. Set aside fifteen minutes to identify a moment when someone physically touched you in a warm and loving way. Relive this moment by remembering the circumstances and the sensory details in as much detail as you can. Relax into the memory, knowing deep in your body that you have been loved and cared for.

"To Sacrifice or Not to Sacrifice," That is the Question

MEDITATION

Present your bodies as a living sacrifice,
holy and acceptable to God,
which is your reasonable act of worship.

Romans 12:1–2

"Sacrifice" can be a loaded word in our culture. To sacrifice is to give up something valued for the sake of something else we consider more important or worthy. It is an act of surrender that may invoke acts of devotion or even martyrdom. Too often, we erroneously consider sacrifice to include the loss of one's inner truth or perspective, simply for the sake of superficially keeping the peace. Especially when applied to our sexuality, the idea becomes problematic particularly when it is gendered with the expectation that those assigned as females make sacrifices of more significance. Women's sacrifices often consist of doing what others want. This can lead to giving less than enthusiastic or even coerced consent for sexual behaviors. So how shall we present our bodies as a living sacrifice as the apostle Paul suggests?

Working with a passage often translated as "present your bodies as a living sacrifice, holy and acceptable to God" (Romans 12:1–2), Eugene Peterson, a theologian and pastor, removes those negative connotations of sacrifice in his biblical paraphrase in The Message: "So here's what I want you to do, God helping you: Take your everyday, ordinary life—your sleeping, eating, going-to-work, and walking-around life—and place it before God as an offering. Embracing what God does for you is the best thing you can do." In Peterson's paraphrase, can we understand what God does for us as including giving us bodies that love to absorb new sights, sounds, and tastes; bodies that love to be caressed and appreciate being seen and valued by others? Expanding a sexually positive narrative into The Message version might say, "Take your everyday, ordinary sensual and sexual life—your sleeping alone and with others, eating crunchy apples and gulping ice tea on a hot summer day, going to work in the quiet of your car or by walking through nature, and making love and caressing a beloved—and place it before God as an offering. Embracing all of life's sensual gifts that God gives to you is the best thing you can do." When we rest in the knowledge of being abundantly loved within our fully sensual and sexual bodies, this is our gift to God. We bring ourselves just as we are. We present our bodies in our holy, everyday, sensual walking-around life as a gift to God. That is our offering. It is our gift. It is enough. And we offer it up as sacrifice.

> *Giver of Blessings, when we deprive ourselves and sacrifice in unhealthy ways to earn your praise we make the spiritual journey spiritless. Help us focus instead upon the gifts of life that you have abundantly given. Open our eyes to your gift of a joy-filled sensual life.*

REFLECTION

1. Experiential activity:
   a. Stop what you are doing. Close your eyes and just smell. Do this until you can smell three different odors. Just smell.
   b. Next, tune into your ears and, with eyes closed, pick out three different sounds. Just listen.

2. What is one thing you do every day in your "going-to-work and walking-around life" that is boring to you? As you consider this activity, ask yourself what sounds, smells, visuals that surround you during its performance? What is the feel or touch of things as you engage in this activity? Does being attentive to the senses relieve the boredom?
3. If you knew God's desire was for your gratitude for the sensual gifts in your life, what do you consider those gifts to be? If nothing comes to mind immediately, move around your space with an eye for that which brings you joy and delight or comfort to your senses.

Living Sensually Until the End

MEDITATION

See, I am old; I do not know the day of my death.

Genesis 27:2

Isaac knew he didn't have long to live. Nearly blind and already bedridden, he was thinking of his death. What does one do with the realization that the end is near? Isaac asked for the gift of savory food, wine, and the smell and touch of his beloved son. As his body was beginning to fail him, Isaac delighted in using his remaining senses by eating a favorite meal in the presence of a beloved person, touching and inhaling his presence.

Few of us know the time of our deaths and neither did Isaac. Yet, his preparation was to stay in the sensual present moment and appreciate it for what it could bring. It is a lesson that reflects the poignancy of the time of endings. For it is not the wealth accrued, the arguments unresolved, or the actions regretted that are on Isaac's mind. It is not the mistakes he made or the accumulated messes he leaves behind. Rather, he chose to enjoy each moment sensually. We don't have to be on our death bed to do the same. To make this gift happen for ourselves is to recognize the immediacy and fragility of our lives. Isaac can show us the way.

> *God of life and of death, the diminishment of our capacities or thoughts of our own death can bring anxiety, fear, depression, or worry. Yet, the gifts of life that can be seen, tasted, smelled, touched, and heard keep us grounded and centered. They open us to appreciate the gift of every moment in each new, special day. Teach us to pay attention. Remind us to open ourselves to the gift that is before us in all its sensual dimensions. Life is good. May we appreciate this not only on our deathbed but right now.*

REFLECTION

1. What are the internal blocks and the external barriers you have for living more sensually? In your journal make a list of these impediments and resolve to begin removing them one at a time. Place a star by each one when you have successfully overcome them.
2. Ask yourself what sensual gift you could experience right here and now. Can you make it happen?
3. What are the sensory experiences you would appreciate if you, like Isaac, were nearing the end of your life? What would be a final meal? Who would you invite to sit with you? What would you want to smell? Since hearing and touch are the last senses to leave us, what would you want to hear and who would you want to touch?

Who is in the Mirror?

MEDITATION

All of us, with unveiled faces, seeing the glory of the Lord as though reflected in a mirror, are being transformed into the same image.

2 Corinthians 3:18

If we were given the assignment to write down ten things we do not like about our body, most of us could do that in record time! However, if asked to write down ten things that we like about our body, the assignment becomes much more difficult and, for too many, impossible. Why is this such a common phenomenon? We could begin counting the number of industries and businesses that depend on body dissatisfaction and low self-esteem. But few of us ever consider that a negative critique of our bodies is an insult to the Creator who pronounced all of creation as good, including our bodies. All body negativity distracts from our ability to treasure both the beauty and miracle that we all are. We can, however, replace our dissatisfaction with wonder at these incredibly miraculous body selves. Every single body is a working miracle. Just breathing in and out 17,280 to 23,040 times every day is a miraculous event! Those of us who live to be eighty will take more than 500 million breaths in our lifetimes!

How we came to these negative views of our bodies is of less importance than the deconstruction of them. This reversal of perspectives is a necessary spiritual practice. After all, we will neither protect nor adequately care for that which we do not treasure or value. It is only by loving ourselves—all of ourselves—that we can, in turn, begin to reflect Goodness. It is only by embracing these miraculous bodies that we will be able to see others as the miracles they are as well. The spiritual call to loving acceptance is to look into the mirror honestly and with unveiled vision, confidently seeing the glory of God reflected back at us.

God in our mirror, we confess we are consumed with ourselves and yet blinded from seeing the miracle that we are. Too often our negativity shields us from seeing our resemblance to you. Remove the veil from our faces and in our very being: in our walking and talking, living and loving, we may reveal to ourselves and others the miracles that reflect your glory. Thank You.

REFLECTION

1. Do you have a body part that does not function? Note the different ways in which you have learned to adapt and accommodate. How are these miraculous feats? Have you ever had a body part that stopped functioning even temporarily? How did healing come about? What made it feel miraculous?
2. Spend at least ten minutes identifying what parts of the human anatomy are the most astonishing to you and then, as if to a child, explain out loud why these body parts or organs are miraculous.
3. Experiential activity: This exercise requires a large towel, sheet, or lightweight blanket that can cover your head and shoulders. In front of a mirror, drape the fabric over your head, symbolizing the faults and foibles and weaknesses that get us into trouble. Consider this a negativity covering. Slowly allow the cover to slip from your head as if a Lover

God or Jesus—is lifting it from you and hear these words as you look into the mirror.

"I am in you and you are in me. We are made in the image of Goodness. Look in the mirror."

Start over and repeat it multiple times until you have a sense of liberation at these assurances.

4. In Greek mythology, Narcissus fell in love with his reflection in a pool of water, unable to eat or drink because of his infatuation. Too often Christians live with the mindset that it is God's will that we do *not* live in love with ourselves. How comfortable are you with the idea of seeing your own beauty in the mirror? Which is easier to believe in, your inner beauty or your outer beauty? Where did this teaching come from?

Stand Tall, Shortcomings and All

MEDITATION

He was trying to see who Jesus was,
but on account of the crowd he could not,
because he was short in stature.

Luke 19:3

We are told that Zacchaeus's body was particularly short. Though he was a rich and powerful tax collector, when it came to simply trying to see above the crowd of people around him, he could not. This short stature may well have created a sense of self-conscious inadequacy. That insecurity may have even led him to choose his job as an employee of the oppressors of his own people. Yet all his money, status, and power were completely useless in overcoming his inability to see over the crowd. Sometimes we want something so badly that we will do just about anything to get it. Zacchaeus was determined. Neither his dignity nor his claim to high status was going to deter him from being a part of what was happening. He wanted more.

So many of us stress out about our body. Are things the "appropriate" size? Will they perform as desired? This misplaced concern and personal insecurity is fueled by businesses with a vested interest in maintaining sexual ignorance and stereotypes because it fuels their profits. Intimacy is never about performance but about relatedness. While an individual's largest sex organ is their skin, the most powerful one is the mind.

So what was Zacchaeus's response to this perceived physical deficit?

I suspect he first removed the expensive jewelry from his soft hands, tied his richly embroidered robes tightly around his waist, and then, with the eagerness of a child, he found the nearest tree and, losing all professional dignity, he climbed it. He vowed that no shortcoming would get in his way. When we accept who we are and refuse to let our perceived deficiencies stand in the way, we step out in faith. Oftentimes when we do, we find, like Zacchaeus, that good things unexpectedly happen.

All-Knowing One, you know how inadequate and critical of our bodies we can feel. Sometimes we are angry at our shortcomings and think "if only . . ." Too often, we focus on what we can't do or what is not going right. Help us accept our bodies and our perceptions of limitations, imperfections, not as obstacles to happiness, but as vessels that hold divine possibilities. Remind us to lift our vision higher, to ask the grander questions of what brings joy and delight. Then, give us courage to use our bodies to seek out our heart's desire.

REFLECTION

1. Experiential activity: Many of us find it very easy to be critical of our body, so stand in front of a mirror and name aloud six things about your body that you like. Say to the person in the mirror,

   "I really like ________ about you."

2. After you have done this, assume what you feel to be a sexy stance while looking in the mirror and repeat the exercise.
3. Do it a third time while still in the sexy pose but this time change the language to first person.

   "I like ________ about *my* body.

4. Now reflect on which body parts were easier to appreciate and which were harder. On a scale of difficulty from one to ten, rate how easy this exercise was to do.
5. Finally, if you feel comfortable, ask someone who supports you and whom you trust to watch as you repeat step #3. Their only job is to watch, not comment. Then tell them how it felt to assume a sexy posture and say these things about yourself in front of them.

Biblical Public Displays of Nudity

MEDITATION

No creature is hidden, but all are naked
and laid bare to the eyes of the one to whom
we must render an account.

Hebrews 4:13

During the Reformation, there was great consternation about public displays of nudity; many of the Reformers took an axe to much of the artwork of their day, aiming for the genitalia. This explains the absence of numerous sculpted penises in museums: they were hacked off by offended Christian men. This repulsion has survived. In 1908, after the completion of Union Station in Washington, DC, statues of the thirty-six nude Roman legionnaires above the rotunda had to have a strategically placed shield installed in front of their genitalia. In 2001, John Ashcroft, the son of a conservative preacher, upon becoming the Attorney General under President George W. Bush, ordered that the exposed bosom of "The Spirit of Justice," a bronze statue at the Justice Department, be completely covered with a drape.

But there is significant nudity in scripture. King David wore very little as he danced for joy before God and the townspeople (2 Samuel 6:14). One of his wives was so incensed by the interest the king attracted among the young slave girls (2 Samuel 6:20–22) that she accused him of being nearly naked. And while Christians may understand that the torturous death of crucifixion included the public nudity of the convicted, few know that the rite of baptism, including that of Jesus (Matthew 3:13–17), was also done in the nude.[12] When Peter jumped into the sea to greet Jesus, he first put on his garment (John 21:7) because fishermen in Jesus's day worked in the nude. Lazarus was wrapped nude in burial clothes so that when the community unwrapped him as Jesus instructed, he would have been exposed (John 11:44). Then there is the scantily-clad young man who, when threatened on the Mount of Olives, escaped with his life by leaving behind his clothing (Mark 14:51). And, of course, the common interpretation of the Genesis story is that embarrassment of nudity caused the first human couple to grab the nearest fig leaf.

Obviously then, the Bible is not skittish about the naked body. In fact, it teaches that all of us stand naked before God in our glorious diversity. Every mole, scar, and wrinkle, every roll of fat, all manner of genitalia, and all seeming imperfections we think we have are all uncovered before God. And guess what? It is all good. It is very good.

Seer of all things hidden, it is scary to know that you see all of us, from our hearts to our genitalia. Help us accept our nakedness as a gift with no need to pretend or justify or defend. Help us be who we are, knowing it is enough and that the body is very good.

REFLECTION

1. What is your relationship to your body? Your friends' bodies? Your lovers' bodies? Is it an easy-going relationship or a conflictual one? Are some parts unknown and waiting for relationship? What kind of a relationship do you want with your body? How can you ask for it?
2. Experiential activity: Stand nude in front of a full-length mirror to view your body. On a scale of one to ten, how comfortable

are you? Stay with those feelings and ask yourself where they came from? Identify the people, teachings, or experiences that shaped your feelings about your nude body, and, if you would like to increase your comfort level, do the following body postures, repeat the statement, and then reflect on it:

a. Raise your hands as if in praise and repeat: "I have one great body, made in God's image. And it is good."
b. Wrapping your arms around yourself, give a tight and affectionate hug and repeat: "My body is a hard-working miracle that is keeping me going the best that it can. And it is good."
c. Hold your arms out wide and repeat: "Here I am, world, I stand unashamed. This body is good enough. I am good enough."
d. Journal your responses and reflections.

Egos and Orgasm

MEDITATION

One thing I have laid hold of, forgetting what lies behind and straining forward to what lies ahead.

Philippians 3:13

Self-forgetfulness is a prerequisite for ecstasy. To forget oneself during moments of intense pleasure means there is no inner audience observing, judging, critiquing. There are no parents, priests or preachers, or politicians present, nor is there a judgmental Father God. If we stay in our heads, we are not forgetting. We are monitoring. Self-forgetting means whatever is, was, or has been happening are all completely laid aside. Bad choices, sexual disasters, previous trauma, or issues with body image as well as children's needs, unmade beds, tomorrow's plans, and menu planning are all forgotten in favor of the joy of this present moment.

But reaching this state of self-forgetting requires the risk of being vulnerable. Vulnerability requires that trust be present—both in ourselves and our partners. We need confidence that we have chosen our partners wisely and that we not only have the language and the ability to state our boundaries and needs clearly, but are assured that they will be honored by our partner. To trust is to feel safe and confident and to be able to say, "no," "not yet," "stop," "this way," "not that way," "more" and "Yes!!!" Trust and vulnerability invite self-forgetfulness, allowing us to listen and respond to our body's sensations. That creates the possibility of ecstasy.

Since our ego tasks include self-protection, it is possible that the noise of thoughts and internal distractions prevent our relaxing into trust and vulnerability. This can be a result of our personal sexual history, the messages with which we were raised, or lack of trust in the relationship with our current partner. When those concerns are appropriately addressed and when we trust and rely on the Sacred Giver of life and pleasure, we can release and relax into the goodness of this bodily moment. Trusting in the goodness of the body's pleasurable senses, we find ecstasy.

Giver of Pleasure, help us move beyond distractions to the trust and vulnerability of sensual and sexual pleasures. Thank you for every pleasurable sensation that excites our spirit with joy and delight. These are your gifts of self-forgetting.

REFLECTION

1. Do a scan of the following impediments to self-forgetting to determine which ones might be more problematic for you:
    a. Daily interferences such as tasks/activities
    b. Issues or conversations of the past
    c. Staying in the present moment
    d. Distrusting your ability to communicate honestly about what you want or need or don't want
    e. Trust that your partner will listen and respond compassionately
    f. Unwillingness to be vulnerable
    g. Others?
2. Thought experiment: When there are past intimacy issues or memories from previous relationships that interrupt your ability to stay in the present moment with vulnerability, imagine those concerns as ghosts flying through the room and buzzing around your ears. Give the concern or memory permission to fly around and then say aloud, "Okay, I hear you but now is not the time to be talking to me. I'll deal with you later. Now go away."
3. Self-forgetting is not the same thing as repression. Sometimes we cannot—and should not—forget because something unresolved is nudging us to address what we are avoiding. Perhaps it is the need for self-forgiveness, forgiveness of others, fear of vulnerability, or changes in your expectations. Make a resolution to address this by talking it out with a trusted friend and, if needed, seek professional help from someone who knows how to help you heal so you can move on uninhibited.

Shameful Taboos

MEDITATION

I shall not be put to shame.

Psalm 119:6

In some households, it is taboo to talk about women's monthly cycles. Menstruation is considered a topic only for women to discuss. This carefully controlled secret then becomes a taboo covered in shame: messy, painful, scary, or bloody. In opposition to this taboo, we should consider menstruation as the mark of fertility that announces we are sexual beings. Menstrual rhythms synchronize with the cycles of the moon and, when they stop, new life may come forth.

Jesus did not recoil from a hemorrhaging woman, though religious practice of the day told him that her presence made him unclean and unfit to enter holy places. Rather, Jesus welcomed social intercourse with women and others whose very "impure" lives put their entire lived existence on the outside. Jesus did not honor cultural standards. Further, we can safely assume there are no taboos in the realm of God. Why? Because when and where Love prevails there are no shameful secrets about gender, gender identity or expression, orientation or our basic biological physicality. Can we believe it? For where Love is, God is. And where God is, shame cannot exist. Think on these things and believe in a love without taboos. Then, discard all shame.

Shameless One, we confess that we compare our bodies with others and too easily find ourselves deficient. Help us live without shame, never sinking into the abyss of not-good-enough. Forgive us when we refuse to believe that your love covers our real and imagined deficiencies. Forgive us for refusing to believe that our bodies are gifts from you just as they are. Help us remember that you honor and bless the earth's fertility and our own. Then, teach us to live without shame.

REFLECTION

1. Experiential activity: With a pen and paper, give yourself five minutes to write a list of shameful taboos in your family and the wider culture.
   a. Then assume a body pose that expresses shame to you as you read each line. Take note of how that makes you feel emotionally and physically.
   b. Next, assume a confident body pose. As you reread the list, repeat the following statements after each one and then slowly rip the paper until only small pieces of remain:
   - There are no taboos in God's house
   - There is no shame in God's presence
   - Love and shame cannot co-exist
   - I choose love, not shame
   - God is shameless
   - I refuse to be ashamed
   - I am not ashamed
2. Experiential Activity: Do you have a shameless God? Or do you have an image of a God who uses shame to control humanity? If this is a problem to consider, then set up two chairs facing each other. In one chair, imagine a God of love uninterested in shaming anyone and in the second chair a

God of severe judgment who uses shame to punish. Now, moving from one chair to the other, have a conversation between these two "gods." Do this until the conversation resolves itself into some new insights. At the conclusion, consider how it felt to hear your thoughts aloud. What did you learn about your ideas of God? You may want to journal any new insights that emerged from this dialogue.

Breathing Life into Dry Bones

MEDITATION

I will cause breath to enter you, and you shall live.

Ezekiel 37:5

There is something intimate about lying in a lover's arms and synchronizing your breathing. It requires paying close attention to their breath and our own. Often, in the process of becoming attuned to each inhalation and exhalation, the partners will naturally slow their breathing as they feel the rising and falling of the other's torso. This tuning might open the door to an intimate conversation or a calm and peaceful mental state. Or the closeness of it may shift toward an emotional intimacy that precedes physical intimacy. The outcome is not the focus or goal. Rather, it is the practice of becoming as one breathing entity, like the breath of God. How shall we consider God's breath entering our lungs?

God showed the prophet Ezekiel a valley after the trauma of war. The valley was filled with dry bones; it was there that God told Elijah that those skeletons would grow flesh and muscle, breathing on their own as fully rejuvenated bodies. The breath of God can lead to resurrection, a reassembling of our embodied selves. How shall we open ourselves to this hopeful message? How do we open ourselves to the intimacy of God breathing with us and through us, reviving us and bringing us to life? As with our partner, perhaps it begins by paying attention, slowing our own breath as we listen, feeling the presence of this Breath of Life.

> *Breath of Life, blow your love through us. Sing through us the music of love and compassion. Fill us with songs of justice and freedom. Forgive us when we push you away, forgetting that you are our Source, the very Source of our breath. You give us life. You give us breath. Slow us down, quiet the tension and panic of our breathing that we may listen more closely to our beating hearts, breathing in unison with you.*

REFLECTION

1. Experiential Activity: Make three columns on a piece of paper and write the name of someone who has loved you at the top of each column. Under each name, list at least three ways they expressed their love for you. You may wish to fill each column with memories of the ways you were/are loved by each individual. If you can find photos of yourself at the age when you were the closest to them, attach one to the bottom of each column. Cut apart the columns with scissors and tape the ends of each one together to create bracelets. Now when you feel like dried-up bones with little value, consider the love expressions on these bracelets. Slip one or all three of these bracelets on your wrists as a symbol of love memories in your life. May it represent God blowing the flesh back into your soul, reconnecting your body with love.

2. Experiential Activity: Choose one of the three photos from the first exercise and have a conversation. First, voice any feelings of want. Perhaps you feel dried up or flat. Then hear the photo talk back to you, recalling aloud the times and ways there is life around you and in you, with affirmation, support, and love. Reassemble any "dried bones" you may be feeling in conversation between your weary self and your loved self until you can remember the life of love that is yours to claim. Close by rereading the "Breath of God" prayer.

Loving a Nurturing Mother and Sexual God

MEDITATION

From my birth I have leaned upon you,
my protector since my mother's womb.

Psalm 71:6

Millenia before Christianity, those who followed women-centered religions created art and figurines of their goddesses that emphasized often-ponderous breasts and wide child-bearing hips, accentuating what they considered to be the profound wonders of fertility. Rather than hiding these fecund parts of the female in their sacred life, they admired, respected, and honored them. This status is portrayed in at least two female postures. At the so-called Palace of Knossos in Crete, archeological fragments were reassembled to reveal a shapely female wearing a gown fashioned to intentionally display her bare breasts. Both of her arms are uplifted as if in a moment of praise while she, bare breasted, holds a snake aloft in each hand.[13] A second posture found in African archeology is of a woman who stands cupping both of her naked breasts, unashamed. Her posture appears to offer to the observer a reminder that survival depends on the breasts: symbols of female nurturance and the power of motherhood. For us, both these postures accenting breasts and the nurturance they offer may seem odd. In our culture, breasts are sexualized rather than honored as life-giving symbols, while fertility and motherhood are given lip service rather than valued through paid family leave, affordable child care, and equal pay.

Yet, both these goddess postures convey what we might consider a paradox: vulnerability and strength. Whether opening and uplifting the arms to reveal bare breasts or cupping them to draw attention, both postures reflect the unashamed vulnerability of giving and nurturing life. Vulnerable yet powerful. The strength of these life-givers who gaze back at us through the ages is palpable. They know the power of their sexual, life-giving bodies and they stand bare-breasted, displaying them.

Abundant Mother God, you give birth to us, feed us, and nurture us along life's journey. You give us life and show us that being sexual is who we are. Our bodies hold no shame in your eyes. Indeed, your love models how to nurture one another. Birther of humanity, help us stand confidently in our bodies. May we vulnerably give life to others and without shame mother a hurting world.

REFLECTION

1. Experiential Activity: Place a soft rug or blanket on the floor or bed and rest your head on a small pillow as you curl into a fetal position. Now, gently rock your body and imagine that the arms of Mother God are cradling you. What does She say

to you? What reassurances does She give? What song is She singing to you? If this is difficult, ask yourself why and journal your response.

2. One of the names for God in Hebrew scripture is "el Shaddai." It is usually translated as God Almighty. But because it may mean "mountainous" and is usually linked to fertility, some scholars suggest the word could be translated faithfully as "the Breasted one." Can you envision the comfort of cuddling at the breast of God?[14] Turn to your journal and write about your comfort or discomfort with that image.
3. Experiential Activity: There is nothing about our bodies that is shameful to God. That means there is no body part that is undeserving of praise. Identify which body part is the most difficult for you to accept lovingly, perhaps because of ridicule, trauma, or a comparison to some idealized image. Hold that body part in your hands and imagine offering it to a loving Mothering God. What will She do with it? How does She respond?

When Life Happens—The Aging Journey

MEDITATION

I will sing to the Lord because (God)
has dealt bountifully with me.

Psalm 13:6

There is a truism among elders that sounds fanciful to a child. They say: "The older I get, the faster time goes." This is a common experience, so what do we do when we wake up one morning and realize that others see us as elderly? While we may not see ourselves this way, the body does send signs: decreased energy, aches that were not there before, changes to our libido. This is especially problematic when, with age, our bodies lose elasticity and stamina along with libido. Our ability to meet culturally driven, gendered expectations of sexual performance and response may change, lessen, or seem to disappear. Without an intentionality to infuse our erotic lives with curiosity and risk-taking, boredom can easily set in, leading to disappointment and unfulfillment. Now what? Because in our society aging people are not expected to have a sex drive, or want, or need one, we are uncomfortable connecting the elderly with the erotic. Now what? Indeed!

If we have absorbed a cultural definition that sexuality is primarily about orgasm, then an aging body with reduced energy or no relational outlet is a problem. If, however, in the intervening years we have discovered sexuality is about the ecstatic joy of pleasure, both sensual and sexual, then aging can be a matter of adjustment to changes rather than a mourning of loss. After all, some of our senses actually deepen with time. Just as in the middle adult years of parenting and career, we adjust to scheduling erotic time instead of the spur-of-the-moment, spontaneous encounters of our youth, so in our aging years, sexual expression shifts again, this time toward deeper connection and intimacy, possibly becoming more sensual and relational than orgasmic. The erotic life is not measured in orgasms but in connections. It is not less than, but different from.

While the book of Genesis is not known as factual history (it is highly unlikely that Noah fathered three sons at the grand age of 500 [5:32], built an ark and endured a catastrophic flood at 600, or that a post-menopausal Sarah [18:11] nursed a newborn son [21:7] whose father was 100 years old) those myths contain truths: God is not finished with us until our dying breath. As righteous people, we continue building the realm of God "on earth as it is in heaven" by loving as we are loved, treating others as we would be treated, and praising and joyfully affirming the goodness of all sensual gifts of life until our last breath. Pleasure is here, now, in this present moment, and can be found at whatever age. Ours is simply to keep our aging eyes open, give praise wherever it is found, and wait expectantly as the Divine Creator winks at us in appreciation. Then in humble praise we sing of the goodness of every intimate touch and each intimate exchange until the very last note of our lives moves into eternity.

Alpha and Omega, our Beginning and End, change is difficult and we often approach our future with fear and trepidation. Remind us of your constancy now and always. Remind us of the durability and sensuality of Love Without End.

REFLECTION

1. A thought experiment: Imagine standing at the pearly gates of heaven after death and discovering that the entrance exam was to name the best pleasurable experience you ever had. What story would you tell?
2. Name three understandings you have now that were outside your capabilities when you were younger.
3. What is the one piece of wisdom you have now that you lacked earlier that could have made a difference in your life? Is there a younger person in your life who might welcome hearing this?
4. In one sentence, what line of a song have you been given to sing to the world?

Intimacy with a Lover God

MEDITATION

O Lord, you have searched me and known me.

Psalm 139:1

The Hebrew word "yada" is translated "to know" in English. It has a wide range of meanings, but one meaning expresses intimacy, as in the erotic intimacy of "Abraham knew Sarah." There is a depth to this knowing. Under this intimacy of knowing is the understanding of the strong bond of a covenant as when God "chooses" (yada) Abraham (Genesis 18:19). So with this meaning in mind, what would happen if we understood that God has searched us and knows (yada) and loves us as intimately as a lover might? What if we accepted that this Love moves toward us with a sacred covenant of lovemaking throughout our lives? If the Creator knows us so intimately as to see us being formed in the womb (Psalm 139:13), then surely our bodies are known inside and out—even more intimately than a lover would know the curves of our bodies. Would a Lover God be critical of our bodies? Would a Lover God enroll us in a "30 Days to a Better Body" program? Or would this Lover God who hears the sighs of our heart, our deepest pains, and our highest dreams not treat us gently? Hold us carefully? Respond with loving kindness and acceptance? Would a Lover God move to comfort us in our physical suffering? And, if so, would this Lover God also not playfully nudge us to move toward the abandoned delight of self-forgetting in orgasmic joy?

Lover God, it is scary to think how well you know us with nothing hidden from you. You move toward us always for our good, always pouring out your love to us in these bodies. Help us to be unafraid of our vulnerability before you. Teach us in your intimate ways to trust in the goodness of our sensual and sexual bodies. Thank you for the overflowing Love you have toward us. Thank you for the binding covenant to love us until our final breath of air. You are our excellent lover. We are deeply blessed to be known so deeply.

REFLECTION

1. A thought experiment: Imagine lying nude in a secluded and private place where no one would ever disturb you. You lie comfortably in the sunshine, feeling the breeze on your skin. Now, as you are completely relaxed, imagine that the gentle breeze on your skin is God exploring, caressing, and taking delight in your body ever so lightly. Imagine the sun's warmth on your skin as the breath of God hovering close as evidence of God's protective presence.
2. If you can, imagine what words a Lover God would say to you.
3. If the image of God as Lover is troublesome for you, think about your own relationships with God and with others. Is it possible to be in a deep covenant, divine or earthly, without a level of intimacy?

Trust Like a Child

MEDITATION

Unless you change and become like children,
you will never enter the kingdom of heaven.
Matthew 18:3

Almost all of us are mesmerized watching children lost in laughter. Giggling and shrieking with delight, they lose themselves in the joy of the moment, often collapsing in pure happiness. When children feel safe, they can more easily step into joy. When adults trust in faith, we, too, can feel safe. And this may lead us to the outrageous laughter and risk-taking behavior of children. Here are some Christian faith truisms to consider:

- Love always wins over fear, so why be afraid of trying something new?
- Grace always offers forgiveness and acceptance, so why live timidly?
- Death never has the last word in the cycle of life, birth, death, and rebirth, so why live cautiously?
- There is no enemy who is not also our sibling, so why refuse to befriend them?
- There is no experience that God cannot use, so why not take a risk and step out in faith?
- There is no limit to the abundance of God's love and grace, so why not live courageously?

With these promises, we can dare to take risks. Just as surely as a child will fearlessly leap into the waiting arms of a loving parent, so faith trusts that the love of the Divine will catch us every time. Trust leads to freedom and freedom moves us into joy and delight. How? It's about trust. Children know this. Trust like a child.

O Playful One, you call us to leave the sidelines huddled in fear. You call us to play in this playground of life that you set before us. We play in these bodies in ways that bring delight and comfort and joy and pleasure. May laughter be our response to such goodness. May our delight in our bodily experiences be our offering of gratitude. Teach us to risk. Teach us to trust as a child and may our laughter be our prayer of thanksgiving.

REFLECTION

1. Find a place where you can observe children at play. Notice the ways they trust those around them to keep them safe. Notice the chances they take when they trust that they won't be hurt. Notice how they take risks just to see what will happen.
2. Identify something that would bring you joy but that would require some risk-taking on your part. It could be asking someone you don't know well to meet you for coffee, or offering a compliment to a stranger, or dancing to a favorite song or twirling under a tree in a park. Then, do it!
3. If you find trust to be difficult, write out a prayer about this struggle. Then, with your non-dominant hand, write a response from the Sacred that reassures you. If there is no reassurance at first, simply respond with your dominant hand and make it a conversation. Do this until you sense a resolution or a spiritual insight.

Childhood and Sensual Play

MEDITATION

And a little child shall lead them.

Isaiah 11:6

Have you ever watched a young child at play? Children are naturally curious about this amazing world and their bodies—and the bodies of others, for that matter. It is through their senses that they discover and learn. I have watched in amazement as a baby first discovers their toes, puts them in their mouth, and sucks on them, because it feels good.

I have watched in amusement (and one mother's deepest mortification) when a little boy fondled himself on the church's stage while singing in the children's choir during worship, because it felt good.

I remember as a preschooler getting naked and burrowing myself into a twelve-inch hole of warm sand where I discovered that the deeper I buried myself, the cooler it felt on my bottom. The temperature change and soft abrasion against my skin felt good.

Children naturally and eagerly explore and discover the wonders of this creation with its astonishing sensuality of smells, tastes, touches, sights, and sounds, including their bodies and genitalia. This is how children learn about the goodness of life. Even the smallest child is guided by their senses. It is natural and it often feels good. We can learn much about sensuality from children: Be curious. Reach for it. Discover and learn.

Let those with ears hear.

O Marvelous Creator, thank you for this world that we explore through our various senses. With each new sight, touch, smell, taste, and sound, our hearts expand in wonder at all you created. Our bodies' senses are a miracle. Forgive us when we are too busy to notice. May we become as children, open to wonder.

REFLECTION

1. Think about childhood sensual experiences of your life. What were the sounds or smells that intrigued you? What new things were you excited to see and explore? Notice that these questions are about sensual, physical, bodily experiences, not necessarily overtly sexual experiences.
2. How did the adults around you respond when, as a child, you wanted to explore those sensual things that were not allowed? Was your curiosity encouraged or restricted?
3. If, in your memories, you recall admonishments not to touch or explore your body, how did that make you feel? What lessons did you learn from that experience? Now, write a letter in your journal to yourself as a child but from someone who wants to protect and teach about the body while encouraging curiosity.

Faith Outside the Lines

MEDITATION

Why are you talking about having no bread?
Do you still not perceive or understand?

Mark 8:17

Jesus told his followers to beware of the "yeast" of religious professionals, but they thought this was a criticism for having running out of bread (Matthew 16, Mark 8). Astonished, Jesus couldn't believe what he was hearing and reminded them they had evidence to the contrary. They had evidence of the miraculous abundance of loaves and fishes, but because they still did not trust in God's sufficiency, they became self-critical. Their lack of trust turned to self-blame and self-reproach and an inward turn. Trust requires that we keep our eyes focused outward toward that which holds us fast: the abundance of God's steadfast love and goodness.

To follow Jesus and to trust in God's goodness, we must see and remember the miracles before us. This will keep us living deeper, fuller lives. What would happen if we gave up self-blame and instead kept our eyes on the One who is completely trustworthy? Would we begin to take risks to love more extravagantly? To ask for what we want? To explore? To be curious? Would this not lead to flourishing lives?

Our faith that trusts in goodness does not conform to harmful social rules about the body, nor does it require obedience to rigid boundaries about gender or gender roles. Faith is not about coloring inside the lines out of fear that we might upset God if we don't. God is already on our side and is not contained by our petty lines.

We cannot be separated from Love (Romans 8:38–39). It is okay to color outside the lines if that is where we are most authentic and real, if that is where we will do no harm.

The path of faith is often outside the lines because, by definition, faith is never about playing it safe. It is about following Love into new ways of being, new visions of who we could be, new vistas of possibility, knowing "all things are possible" (Matthew 19:26). By trusting in goodness, we can free ourselves to risk a radical investment in life, in community, and the gifts of sensual and sexual pleasure.

Wise and Patient One, forgive us when we say we trust you but live fearful of your impatience or anger. Give us a resolve to love with more abandon, to live more fully, and to risk more courageously in your name. May we trust you more so your will may be done on earth as it is in heaven.

REFLECTION

1. On a risk-taking scale of 0 to 100 (0 is extremely distrustful with no risk-taking, 100 is extremely foolhardy and trusting everybody, and 50 is the solid center of considering evidence of trustworthiness and being willing to trust your own truth by taking the important risks):
   a. Rate your willingness to take risks in the following areas:
      Financial _____ Physical _____ Emotional _____
      Sexual _____ Spiritual _____
   b. Tease out the conditions for trust and mistrust in each of these categories.
2. What evidence do you have in your life that the Creator can be trusted and what makes you skittish and mistrusting of such a claim if applied to your sexually intimate life?

3. Which of the following psalms would help you find a strong trusting center to counter self-reproach and self-blame for being a sexual person?
   a. Trust in the Lord and do good; live in the land and enjoy security. (Psalm 37:3)
   b. I trust in the steadfast love of God forever and ever. (Psalm 52:8)
   c. In God I trust; I am not afraid. What can a mere mortal do to me? (Psalm 56:11)
   d. . . . because they had no faith in God and did not trust [God's] saving power. (Psalm 78:1)
   e. I shall have an answer for those who taunt me, for I trust in your word. (Psalm 119:42)
   f. Trust in the Lord with all your heart, and do not rely on your own insight. (Proverbs 3:5)

Belly Laughs of Healing

MEDITATION

Our mouth was filled with laughter.

Psalm 126:1

Years of alienation with one son and the recent death of his other son had taken its toll when a friend of mine underwent brain surgery. After drilling holes in his skull to place a shunt to drain accumulated fluid, the doctors were confident of a full recovery. They soon discovered that, not only had the hesitant and lurching walk stopped, but he could now dance in the kitchen with his partner. But it was only when he started laughing that his partner knew that all would be well.

Six weeks after the procedure, when he was recovering, he heard a quip and began to laugh. It was a deep and long laugh that came from the deepest reaches of his belly. He had not laughed like this for a long time. And he laughed and he laughed and then collapsed into giggles, lots of them. What a blessing. What a relief. What a miracle to observe and to feel. His body had responded to the physical intervention. With those difficulties put aside, at least for a time, now the healing of his spirit had begun.

Joyful One, remind us of the importance of laughter to ease our stress and aid in the healing of our bodies and our spirits. Help us surrender to a belly laugh, a gift when it arrives. It is not only righteous living but the full enjoyment of our lives that You are waiting to see. Accept our gift of giggles as our thanks to you. Give us joy, like a belly laugh, a joy that comes from the deep caverns when we may remember all will be well.

REFLECTION

1. When did you laugh until the tears came? Can you think of times when you or others were so sad that uncontrollable laughter erupted as an escape valve or defense mechanism?
2. The poet Kahlil Gibran wrote that, "the deeper that sorrow carves in your being the more joy you can contain." In what ways does sorrow open you to others, to yourself, and perhaps to God?
3. Belly laughs come from deep inside the body. But we will have no such laughter if we are unwilling to be vulnerable about how we look and sound: Loud raucous screaming shrieks, shaking torsos, contortion of our face, and tears

streaming. How comfortable are you with your own uncontrollable laughter in front of others? In the presence of a beloved? In the presence of your faith community? Recall the times when you have been seized with laughter and remember how you felt afterwards.

4. Your assignment is to make a fun and outrageous plan that will delight you and surprise and provoke laughter for you and someone else today. Note the level of stress in your body before and after the laughter.
5. Religious beliefs are often held with seriousness. That was not always, however, the religion of Jesus. Imagine Jesus invites you to a party this evening where there would be fun, riotous games, and beverages of your choice. What jokes would you tell? How would Jesus create a delight-filled evening for those in attendance? And, if this is a difficult assignment examine why this is so.

Finding Joy without J.O.Y.

MEDITATION

You are in the Spirit, since the Spirit of God dwells in you.

Romans 8:9

Jesus. Others. Yourself. J.O.Y. This is the order some of us are taught is the correct priority to live the Christian life. It puts ourselves last and God first—or rather Jesus, since J.O.Y. works better than G.O.Y. This J.O.Y. ladder deemphasizes ourselves and, by implication, our bodies as well. But regardless of the acronym, as an ongoing practice, always putting ourselves last is not psychologically healthy, and good spiritual health is always good psychological health. The life of the spirit is not hierarchical. It is not about who is more important and gets the priority. Neither is there a "bottom" to such a "ladder of importance" because there is no such ladder in the spiritual life. This "ladder" keeps us focused on our inferiority and God/Jesus/Spirit at a distance from our lowly place—a teaching that violates the truth of Jesus as fully human and fully divine.

The God/Spirit we glimpse through Jesus's life and ministry is not found high above, outside, or far away, but rather inside, permeating our bodies, guiding our decisions, loving us, teaching us to love ourselves, inspiring us to love in concrete ways those around us—neighbors as well as enemies. Because it is in our physicality that we live, it is more helpful to integrate the spirituality of God or Jesus within our frail bodies and in our own lived experience. In such an arrangement, God/Jesus/Spirit loves and is love and our response can only be to love. Not because others are more important or have priority but because we are experiencing the indwelling of "godness" within. By discarding this priority ladder and integrating God/Spirit/Jesus inside our fleshly bodies, we are freed to find real joy.

Indwelling Love, it is hard to believe the power of your Love is inside us, for we are fallible. Yet, we are humbled that love and righteousness come through these bodies. We are thankful you do not desire that we think of ourselves as being less important than others. May your power in these bodies free us to freely be.

REFLECTION

1. Self-love can be incredibly difficult, so consider this quote from Christian mystic Meister Eckhart: "Every single creature is full of God. Every single creature is a book about God." What is

your reaction to such an idea? If it is negative, journal a conversation between you and the mystic. If your life is a book about God, what is the God lesson you hope people see in you?

2. Experiential Activity: Body work (if you are able):
   a. Squat or crouch with your hands and knees on the floor. In this position, remember the times and ways you have been told that you are less important, you don't count, are inferior to others, or are a lowly sinner. Those who told you or taught you this may have the best of intentions, but it creates scarring. As you slowly stand, acknowledge these messages and the messengers by saying, "Thanks, but no thanks. That is unhelpful in my spiritual life."
   b. Second position: Move to a chair and sitting with your hands turned upwards consider, "On the one hand I..." (lift one hand to acknowledge your humanity—that is, those things you are working to change to reflect a better version of yourself...) Then lift the other hand upward and say, "And, on the other hand..." (acknowledge those parts of yourself that you and others appreciate). State a sentence for each hand: On the one hand, an acknowledgment of the attributes you hope to attain in your spiritual life, and on the other hand, appreciation for who you are.
   c. Third position: Stand tall stretching your arms over your head. Repeat,

      "I am bigger than I can see
      More courageous than I can imagine
      More loved than I deserve."
   d. Fourth position: Now put your hands on your heart. Repeat,

      "I am big enough, courageous enough, loved enough
      to reveal Love that is in me,

Love that is beside me,
Love that is above me. Amen"

Loving Body Smells

MEDITATION

And the man and his wife were both naked,
and were not ashamed

Genesis 2:25

I don't remember the first time someone slapped my hands when, as a child, I touched my genitals, but I am quite sure that someone did. However, it was conveyed, the message for many of us was that there was something "nasty" about doing so. As a child, I concluded that it must be because of smells that came from that area of my body. As an adult, I learned that some are particularly sexually responsive to aromas. It is called olfactophilia. How was it determined that a particular aroma is a "bad" smell or a "good" one? Smells simply are, right? Some pleasing. Others? Not so much. And, relatedly, how have naturally occurring odors from our bodies come to be labeled shameful? Surely the Creator's pronouncement of "very good" included smells.

We may have also learned that it is bad to touch ourselves lest we have these deliciously pleasant responses. The disastrous conclusion is that such wonderful responses arising from our biology are somehow bad, wrong, or sinful. The pleasure of our body is named as someone else's prerogative and not our own to enjoy. In other words, these are shameful feelings when related to genitalia. Yet, feelings just are. The Creator made us to be human and that means we respond to different sensual and sexual stimuli. Although the first earth creatures were naked and not ashamed as they walked with the Creator each day, various cultures throughout the centuries have taught that sensual and sexual feelings are bad and shameful if not controlled and restricted. Fortunately, Jesus was not of that ilk.

The wisdom of children, before they are taught differently, reveals that sensual (or sexual) body experiences can bring delight and joy. In fact, if we can't appreciate our senses, we can't fully appreciate sexual intimacy either. Good feelings generated in our bodies are to be savored. It is insulting the Creator to suggest such deliciousness is a mistake! As Christian theologian James B. Nelson wrote, "If we do not know the Gospel in our bodies, we may not know the Gospel."

God of All That Is Sensual, thank you for all the wonderful smells that invite us to move outside ourselves. Forgive us when we have labeled the natural parts of being human as sinful rather than seeing this as evidence of your intention for us. Teach us to appreciate our body's capacity to take it all in - in wonder and delight as a child.

REFLECTION

1. Of our five senses, which do you most appreciate? Which is the most troublesome for you?
   a. Taste
   b. Smell
   c. Sound
   d. Sight
   e. Touch
2. Take fifteen minutes to go in search for a special smell.

3. Find a new taste: a new recipe, a different vegetable, food from a culture that is new to you, a dish you've never ordered at a café or restaurant. How comfortable are you with stepping out of the familiar zone of taste? How curious? How resistant? Why or why not?
4. Find a new sound: listen to a musical artist outside your usual listening habits or listen to a different social media channel. How comfortable are you with stepping out of the familiar zone of sound? How curious? How resistant?

Here Comes Pleasure

MEDITATION

So Sarah laughed to herself, saying, '
After I have grown old . . . shall I have pleasure?'

Genesis 8:12

Giving birth at the advanced age of ninety is a hilarious idea, not to mention a daunting one! But in the biblical story, Sarah not only laughed out loud at this preposterous idea, but her follow-up question implies that this was not just about the experience of unusual baby-making but one of pleasure itself: the pleasure of more acceptance from her community, of cuddling a longed-for infant; the pleasure of a complete, but welcomed, disruption to her routine and surprising future; and, of course, the pleasure of increased intimate bonding with her spouse. One wonders: had her pleasure ended long before this? Was she relishing the idea and laughing in the anticipation that she might have sexual pleasure once again? Maybe this prediction of her outlandish procreation would once again put pleasure back on the table, or rather, back in the bedroom.

A procreative bias has a long history throughout Christendom. Over the years, the church has implied that, but for the pressing need for procreation, sexual pleasure was a bad idea. By the second century, St. Clement of Alexandria wrote that "to indulge in intercourse without intending children is to outrage nature."[15] Sexual activity had to be justified for procreation only, not pleasure. But if this is the case, sex becomes an obligation. Is it any wonder that some women welcome post-menopausal years when procreative possibilities cease? Or that contraception is so strongly denigrated by some Christians? How does one have pleasure if sex is marital and primarily focused on procreation? Why can't pleasure be a gift of the Creator? It certainly enhances our life experience.

So, yes, Sarah laughs and keeps laughing. If we so choose and when the time is right, we may all have the delight of toe-tingling primal release that comes from abandoned sexual play, whether alone or with others. The pleasure of this "laughing time" touches our spirit and connects us to something beyond ourselves, whatever our age. While it is true that some fertile bodies are designed for procreation, all of us are designed for pleasure!

O Laughing One, thank you for reminding us that life is good. Thank you for the pleasures that bring unexpected delight and joy. Thank you for the gift of others to share these delightful times with us. Open us to the laughter that comes from pleasure and we will praise your name in public and private places. Oh God, yes! We give you praise.

REFLECTION

1. For many, the access to and availability of contraception disrupts the idea of "sex is only for procreation." For some, resistance to contraception reveals their discomfort with the legitimacy of sexual pleasure for its own sake. What fears do you have, if any, of what would happen if all sexual acts held no religious or political significance?
2. What if the directive, given to the first humans upon leaving the Garden of Eden, to "be fruitful and multiply" (Genesis 1:28) was understood to include the overt subtext to go into the world and make love? How would that change your faith?
3. How might you imagine a verse to follow the Creator's pronouncement that creation was very good (Genesis 1:31)? "And the Creator said, 'Now, let there be abundant pleasure that all of creation may know joy. And may the hills and valleys resound with laughter.'" Would such a verse be compatible with your understanding of the Creator? If not, why not?
4. Choose something sensually pleasurable to do today because your Creator has commanded it. And may you know joy!

No Apologies

MEDITATION

Mary has chosen the better part,
which will not be taken away from her.
Luke 10:42

Mary sits at the feet of Jesus. She is aware that women are to know their place, serving men whether in the kitchen or the bedroom, rather than sitting at the feet of teachers along with men. She risks being criticized and labeled, perhaps viewed as too uppity. Does she try to make herself smaller, shrinking into the shadows so she won't be noticed? Or perhaps she sits close to Jesus, hoping he might protect her from disapproval. Does she have a right to be here?

All of us hear messages intended to squash us, limit the expression of our uniqueness, deny diversity, and prevent dissent. Those who speak up or stand out become targets for criticism. Yet here Mary sits. Waiting. Listening. Learning. Then, when challenged about her decision, Jesus responds, perhaps with an understanding smile, "You have chosen well." In other words, although being who we are without apology may incur a high cost, Jesus encouraged Mary to do just that. Although we are part of a community, our path is our own to choose. Within the context of that community, each of us is a gift that we bring to the realm of God. And in this realm, every voice is heard, every gift valued. Every door is open. Do not be afraid. Walk through it without apology. And know that no one walks alone.

Holy One, thank you for making each of us unique and beautifully gifted for the work of loving this world exactly as you created us to be. We confess that sometimes we can forget our own value, listening to the voices that would sweep us into the shadows. Remind us to be unashamed to live as you desire.

REFLECTION

1. The strongest social pressure is applied to sexual matters, whether it is sexual expression, gender identity, or behaviors. Beginning in early childhood, any deviation from a culture's norms may be derided, shamed, and finally coerced. Similarly, there can be pressure to marry, identify with a binary gender, and become a monogamous, procreative couple, regardless of our interests, skills, or internal compass. There is no scripture that hints Jesus would support any of this, yet plenty of evidence he violated cultural/religious rules. Consider the possibility that you have the freedom to be who you are or want to be sexually and make a list of the sexual or social rules you would like to challenge or disobey.
2. Imagine a conversation with Jesus and Mary, discussing, "Can we have the abundant life you bring, Jesus, without having personal and sexual freedom?" What would Mary say? How would Jesus respond? What do you say?

Free to Be Who I Am

MEDITATION

I am who I am.

Exodus 3:14

"Just who do you think you are?" is a put-down implying that we are acting in inacceptable ways. Translation: "Don't be so different." The subtext may be that we are out of line and will pay a price in the form of criticism or ostracism. Acceptance and belonging are important to humans, but conforming to others' rules means that taking risks is . . . risky.

Our first major step in defining ourselves is usually the discovery of the word "No!" To many parents' dismay, children assert their independence around the age of two, moving from an understanding that "I am your child and a part of you" to "I am my own person!" Just as this is a healthy development for children toward maturity, so is Christian discernment of our own moral path. Many Christians find change or difference in matters of things sexual to be difficult. Conformity, however, ignores the reality that the body of Christ has many parts, each behaving and identifying differently, yet bound in love (1 Corinthians 12:12). Christians do not all think or act the same because the Spirit is not bound by our cultural rules or societal expectations. Led by the Spirit, when we follow our hearts (and conscience), we can freely become who God is leading us to be.

When the Hebrews demanded that Moses verify his message by identifying God's name, we learn God doesn't play that game. God announced, "I am who I am." When we are asked to justify our sexual identity or sexual choices, we don't have to play either. Led by the Spirit as children of God, we are lovingly guided along life's journey by "I am."

Great I Am, our small minds cannot fathom nor our inadequate words contain you. Keep us open to your whisper. And, when we are asked, "Just who do you think you are?" help us to say with confidence, "I am who I am, beloved child of the Great I Am."

REFLECTION

1. Body exercise: "I Gotta Be Me" is an oft-recorded song that expresses the need for individual expression. This sentiment was depicted in a *Far Side* cartoon by Gary Larson, in which a flock of sheep peacefully graze in a pasture while in the very back, a lone black sheep stands on its hind legs bursting into song: "I gotta be me!" Keeping this exuberance in your mind, fold your body into a posture as if you were a closed flower bud waiting to open and whisper three times, "I gotta be me." Then, repeating "I gotta be me" louder each time, slowly allow this flower bud position to open into a posture that conveys confidence. Use all of your body—arms, torso, head, and legs—until you are in a fully confident position. Take in a deep breath as you observe your body and how it feels. Reflect on this exercise. Did it feel authentic? Do you believe it? Whose voice(s) did you hear? Does God approve of your self-confident stance? Why or why not?
2. The children's album "Free to Be You and Me" produced by actress and author Marlo Thomas was named a culturally significant recording by the Library of Congress for its encouragement to children to move beyond the cultural constraints of gender and freely explore who they are and want to

become. Identify ways you may have been limited by gender choices in fashion styles, sports or games, toys, or in choosing a career path or jobs. Who or what experiences encouraged you to expand those limits?

3. With Jesus's approval, Mary stayed in the room to listen to spiritual discussions rather than move to the kitchen with her sister Martha (Luke 10:38–42). If you could violate some restricting or unfulfilling gender norms or expectations, what would they be? Would your God approve of you as Jesus did of Mary?

Who Has Your Power?

MEDITATION

You would have no power over me . . .

John 19:11

Someone is in charge of our body and, if it is not ourselves, then someone else will step in. It is a truism: If we are disempowered, we are also controlled. This happens at a personal level, as exemplified when someone is controlled by a spouse, parent, preacher, or the elders of our congregation or, at a macro level, when cultural ideology and taboos or politicians impose restrictions and control over other adult bodies. When others control bodies without consent, inevitably, some bodies become invisible, trivialized, and sometimes abused and violated. Unfortunately, some religious teachers refer to giving our power over our own body to someone else as God's idea of "honorable submission." The coercive, nonconsensual power over other bodies is not "honorable submission" but abusive power.

A loving Creator gave humanity the freedom to grow and mature into the image of the Divine. The first humans had moral autonomy and personal agency. They had the freedom to decide: Shall we seek knowledge of good and evil? The Creator preferred they stay, yet Love, by definition, always frees us to make our own choices, whether we do so wisely or not.[16] Placing our power and control over our bodily decisions into the hands of another is idolatry, which far too easily leads to power abuse.

The rightness of individual autonomy was affirmed when Jesus commends Mary's unconventional choice to stay to listen to his teachings (Luke 10:38–42) and when the apostle Paul uses the individual's discernment and conscience in making decisions.[17] For Paul, this individual privilege is always taken in light of how one's actions will affect others and how they reflect a loving God (1 Corinthians 10).

We are each invited to find our spiritual way back to the Garden of Earthly Delight as we return to Love. But this can only happen when we honor our agency, find the power to speak, make our own decisions, and live out our own truth.

Abiding Love, it can be easier to let others make difficult decisions for us. We know Love is never invasive but offers freedom to find the path. So guide our lives and give us courage to take the steps needed to move toward your love.

REFLECTION

1. By the age of five, male children learn that "boys" must be tough and not show their feelings while girls learn before puberty that to be a "girl" is to take care of others and not speak their own truth.[18] What lessons did you learn in your

childhood about speaking your truth? Was it welcome? Which feelings were not welcomed? If you identify as gender non-conforming, transgender, nonbinary, or intersex, who in your world has welcomed all of who you are—the truth of your body, your feelings and understanding of yourself? What lessons have you learned?

2. Rate your sense of empowerment on a scale of one to ten, with ten being completely in charge, on the following areas of your life:
   a. finance _____
   b. social relationships _____
   c. political life _____
   d. interpersonal relationships _____
   e. sexuality _____
   f. gender identity _____

3. When others have power over us, especially sexual power, we seldom get what we want or how we want it. Using this 1–5 scale with the following meanings: 1) "I'm hopeless!" 2) "A few times I can eke out a statement but I shy away from it." 3) "Sometimes I can and sometimes not." 4) "Room for improvement but I'm getting better." 5) "I feel empowered most of the time," rate how good you at saying:
   a. "No, that is not what I want. Don't do/say that." _____
   b. "I would like it if you…" _____
   c. "This is what I want/need from you…" _____
   d. "This is my truth and I expect you to honor it." _____
   e. "Your opinion is yours. I do not share it." _____
   f. "I know I agreed but I've changed my mind." _____

Proudly We Wear Our Crowns

MEDITATION

But you, O Lord, are a shield around me . . .
the one who lifts up my head.

Psalm 3:3

Stereotypes distort people's views and opinions so we can't "see" one another. This social conditioning begins young. Racial stereotypes can focus not only on skin color but on any number of other body parts. Nowhere is this more evident than with hair and hair coverings.

Evidence can be seen from the building of the transcontinental railroad when anti-Chinese bigots would cut off the waist-long braided queues of Chinese immigrants and, particularly after the tragedy of 9/11, to the targeting of Sikhs for wearing turbans. Some still feel the need to control the display of natural hair of non-white athletes at sporting events and to outlaw the hijab or the head coverings of many Muslim women. Further, sixty percent of Black girls who attend a white-majority school will experience hair discrimination while in the U.S. work place, eighty percent of Black women say, "I have to change my hair from its natural state to fit in at the office."[19] Unfortunately, these stereotypes are often codified into laws and public policies.

The internalization of negative messages happens far too easily. "Creating a Respectful and Open World for Natural Hair" was introduced in the U.S. House of Representatives in 2021 and passed that house in 2022. It would legislate against discrimination of those with non-European hair textures or styles and, with its acronym CROWN implicitly states that we each have a right to proudly wear the crowns of our unique beauty.

The psalmist writes that God lifts up our heads (3:3). We see that exhibited in a popular internet video depicting friendship between two basketball players of color. As they walk onto the court, the first player is looking down at the ground, his head lowered. The second player, without breaking stride, reaches over gently to lift the chin of his teammate. Surely this illustrates God's action for us lest we yield to the false mirrors of the world.

Do people refuse to see your uniqueness? Your beauty? Do stereotypes prevent an acknowledgement of your legitimate place in the world? Remember who you are and proudly wear the crown, metaphorical or not, that marks you as a child of God. With or without hair, natural or otherwise, you are a gift from the Divine. Be you, without apology.

Protective One, thank you that your view of us is greater than the false images the world projects onto us. Help us resist limitations. Remind us that in your wondrously diverse and beautiful world we, your people, reflect your vision. May we walk tall and in step with how you would have us live.

REFLECTION

1. In what ways has God lifted your head to believe in yourself? Who are the people who have seen you beyond stereotypes?
2. Identify someone you know who may metaphorically have their head down rather than proudly looking out to the world. What would be an affirming message you could convey to gently lift their chin? Can you do it today?

3. At what age did you first hear about body differences? If there was a judgment made about those differences, how would you explain those differences today to someone of that age?
4. Experiential activity: Today, if you are able, take a walk and practice keeping your chin up rather than looking at the ground. Or, if indoors, whether sitting or standing, concentrate on lifting your head and gaze about 45 degrees higher than you usually would. Which feels familiar or natural; looking up or looking down?

Shaking Dust Off Our Sandals

MEDITATION

Wherever they do not welcome you,
as you are leaving that town shake the dust off
your feet as a testimony against them.

Luke 9:5

One wonders what the parents of Peter and Andrew and James and John thought when their sons left the families' fishing occupation to follow a total stranger! They *immediately* left their nets, their livelihood, and their homes (Mark 1:18). Why? Perhaps their response was to the pull of Jesus's invitation and charisma, but it is equally possible their decision was a "push" factor as well. Were they unhappy with the state of their lives? Were they satisfied with fishing day in and day out or was the invitation Jesus offered an opportunity to make a better life, or perhaps find something more meaningful? Were their families dismayed with expressions of consternation or excitement and support? Was leaving their families a matter of desperation or self-preservation?

At the height of the HIV-AIDS epidemic in the early nineties, there were horrible stories of sick people, usually gay men, being kicked out of their families when diagnosed with what was then a terminal illness. Even nearing death, some discovered that neither their pastor nor their congregation would provide spiritual support for them or a funeral. To manage upended lives, many within the sexual minority communities so deeply affected by the epidemic organized casseroles and created meal delivery schedules, held fundraisers to pay the rent, massaged aching limbs, and held round-the-clock vigils and care. It was Love-in-action. Unconditional acceptance. The love and tender care given by this "chosen family" made it obvious where God was. Indeed, many found sacred space at their bedside and in the valley of the shadow of death that this sacred community walked together. Being isolated from their family had not been of their own doing or their choice, yet they had found sacred space, community, and spiritual healing.

We may see parallels in the situations of many gender and sexual minorities. When families are unaware of the breadth of gender diversity or when, out of ignorance or their own woundedness, they put limits on love that require conformity, pain and suffering, and even violence may result. It is important then to move toward healing—to leave hostility and violence behind—trusting that God will provide the community and individuals who can and will embody what grace and love looks like. As Jesus instructed his disciples, we too have permission to shake the dust off our sandals when we are unwelcome and move on. There are pockets of love awaiting us. There are people ready to welcome and embrace all of who we are. And while it is painful to leave some behind, it is also healing to move toward a "chosen family" and be our authentic selves, for where we find love there we will find God.

One in the Shadows with us, it is hard to lose the support of those who are supposed to love and support us, and to push against those we love. Hear our grief and give us courage to seek those places and people where we will find a home with genuine acceptance and unqualified support. In this hospitality may we see you.

REFLECTION

1. There are those who say they love us but have difficulty showing it while others have difficulty acknowledging us. Make a list of those people who see you and accept your path as your own. Think outside traditional circles.
2. Make a second list of people with whom you don't have a strong relationship but who have the capacity to see you in all your fullness. How might you begin to develop a deeper relationship with each one?
3. Examine your heart to ask who you have been judgmental toward? Who do you think needs to change or "straighten up"? Put these names on the top of your prayer list and ask for grace to accept them, their choices, and their life path as their own.
4. Sometimes we envy those who claim their own identity and boundaries because we have difficulty doing so ourselves. Go through the names in the exercise above and ask yourself what they are doing that you have not given yourself permission to do. After prayerful consideration, if you have been judgmental, you may choose to confess this to God or to them and take responsibility for unloving thoughts or actions.

Pushing Back Against Trivialization

MEDITATION

Great is your faith!

Matthew 15:28

Both Matthew and Mark tell a story of a time when Jesus appears to be neither sensitive nor just. The writers begin by noting that it is a foreigner who approaches Jesus. Whether it was her manner or her speech, she is marked as an outsider. Maybe they knew of her or perhaps they were going by appearances. Jesus's apparent stereotyping or racial and ethnic prejudice is confirmed when he very harshly suggests she is a dog (Matthew 15:26, Mark 7:27), suggesting that, as a foreigner, she is of lesser value than those he *really* came to address (Matthew 15:24). The truth of the matter is that his response was exactly what the culture would expect.

But, not to be deterred by other people's assessment of who or what she was, the Canaanite woman stood up to him and made her demand that Jesus take seriously her request to heal her daughter. Her response to being trivialized and dehumanized was to demand that she be noticed and treated as genuine. It is as if she is saying, "Look at me! Do not turn away! I am here as a person in my own right. I deserve healing in my household just like anybody else!" One can imagine that she was not going to leave. She stood her ground and refused to accept the cultural domination that gives some bodies more importance than others. She would not be pushed into a secondary position. Hers was a righteous request and she knew it. And upon hearing this pushback, so did Jesus. His response was to commend her faithful advocacy and to heal her daughter as she had requested. In so doing, Jesus confirms to his followers and us, the readers, that we are not to acquiesce to the hierarchies that trivialize or demean people; that those who stand up for themselves and push back are be commended and applauded. All bodies in all our racial diversities and ethnic subtleties and gendered variations are to be valued and respected. Period.

Powerful One, give us courage to advocate for ourselves, to stand up to the stereotypes and prejudices in our lives. Make us dissatisfied with the status quo and give us the strength to push back against all that is unfair, whether aimed against us or those around us. Understanding that all bodies are sacred, make us radical advocates willing to push back against the values of the world. And may we be unafraid of saying we are wrong whenever we accept the dehumanization of bodies.

REFLECTION

1. On a scale of one to ten, with ten being the highest and strongest advocacy, how well do you advocate for yourself if/when others are dismissive of you or stereotype you?
2. It takes both courage and community to stand up to a culture that dehumanizes people. Who in your community of friends and family would understand and support you when you advocate for yourself and others? Write them a note of gratitude.
3. Make a list of your role models, contemporary or historic, who show(ed) courage in standing up for class or racial justice. Name models for sexual justice and models for body justice.
4. Identify one role model who is particularly courageous and either find a quote by them or summarize in one sentence

how you view their philosophy of courage. Display the quote where you can read it often to give you courage to advocate for yourself and others.

Paul's Model of Gender and Gender Role Flexibility

MEDITATION

Only let us hold fast to what we have attained.

Philippians 3:16

Back in the 1950s, a biologist named Alfred Kinsey, a specialist in the mating habits of wasps began studying human sexuality. He is credited as the first Western scientist to understand that there is a continuum for sexual orientation from fully heterosexual to fully homosexual, with most people being somewhere in the middle. However, it is the continuum of gender that has taken center stage recently, as the gender binary of male and female is being publicly challenged. Other societies and religions have long accommodated a wider view: for example, many Native Americans understood and accepted additional genders, now referred to as two spirit, while ancient Jewish texts identify six genders. Although science supports multiple ways gender can be determined, the idea is too radical for some. In the United States, it is increasingly common for individuals to identify as gender fluid, gender flexible, trans, or gender queer, with a wide variation in how they define their gender roles, identities, and sexual attractions.

While this might seem overwhelming, it appears that the apostle Paul willingly identified himself in a variety of genders and gender roles. To the church of Thessalonica, his gender identity was as a father with his children (1 Thessalonians 2:11) and as a nurse, mostly likely understood as carrying a masculine identity in his day (2:7). Yet, when with the Corinthians, Paul was comfortable thinking as a nursing mother who patiently awaited the time when the children would eat solid foods (1 Corinthians 3:2). And when writing to those in Galatia, Paul spoke of experiencing childbirth with them (Galatians 4:19). The fact that Paul was comfortable switching gender roles in a way that might reflect differing gender identities is instructive. Paul, confident in his call and striving to carry it out authentically, had discarded definitions that others might consider important (Philippians 3:4–6, Romans 11:1). He felt no need to fit into a role or identity if it impeded pursuing that passion of being the person God was calling out. Paul explicitly stated this in his willingness to become all things to all people (1 Corinthians 9:22). Our inner certainty as to who we are cannot be grounded in others' definitions. For Paul, the task of "forgetting the past" and pressing "toward the prize of the heavenly call" (Philippians 3:14) is to hold fast to what we have attained: the status of being beloved children of God.

Many-Spirited One, you call us to you through your son both in history and in the heart, through your Spirit both in us and in the world, through your Creation both in nature and in your creatures, and through your people in all our variations. You are Maker of all, and we hear this heavenly call as we seek to find our home in you.

REFLECTION

1. A gender binary is attractive for some because it is easier: how to act, dress, talk and think are clear. But gender norms can feel like a straitjacket. Make a list of the social norms con-

nected to your gender identity that you find unpleasant (for example, wearing ties as males, shaving your legs as females).

2. Experiential activity: Find a too-small jacket, or use a blanket or rope and sit in a way that somehow binds your body. In this uncomfortable position, slowly read the list you made in response to the prompt above aloud. How does it feel?
   a. Now imagine how it would feel to be a gender other than as you identify. Is it liberating? Confining?
   b. Imagine acting out a gender identity that is different from yours. How comfortable is that imaginative act?
   c. Imagine being misgendered by others rather than being seen as you see yourself. How does it feel?
3. Play with the idea of God as a non-gendered Being and a multi-gendered Being, all at the same time. Is there an advantage to removing or adding a gender identity to God in your prayer life? Use these metaphors when you pray and journal what the experience is like.

Survival as Resistance

MEDITATION

We are surrounded by so great a cloud of witnesses.

Hebrews 12:1

Bible stories often contrast the ways of the unrighteous with the ways of a righteous God. Paul uses the language of the "realm of the flesh" versus the realm of the spirit. The church of Ephesus learned that this spiritual struggle is against both earthly rulers and authorities as well as cosmic forces (Ephesians 6:12). Today, social scientists document the ways structural systems of domination overwhelm through crushing poverty and exploitation of bodies, labor, and indeed, of life itself. In "The Litany of Survival" in *The Black Unicorn*, poet Audre Lorde concludes, "it is better to speak \ Remembering \ We were never meant to survive." Never meant to survive. Writing out of her experience as a Black lesbian, she knew that dominant social structures create a world in which some bodies are not meant to survive. Theologian Katie Geneva Cannon called this a "death-dealing world." Successful domination systems consider human bodies as expendable.

After Jerusalem was destroyed by the dominating empire of their day, the Hebrews sat by the waters of Babylon and wept. There was no music left (Psalm 137). Mary and Joseph faced this death-dealing reality when, after learning Herod was threatening to slaughter all male children, they fled for their lives to a different country (Matthew 2:13–18). For millennia, humans have survived the horrors of body injustice. Jesus's family spent years in Egypt before returning home, while the Hebrews eventually escaped Babylon and did the same.

Through it all, the resilient human spirit resists. Resistance to body injustice is grounded in the deep wisdom of faith that our bodies are worth saving, worth loving and fighting for. Indeed, there is a cloud of witnesses broader than this earthly community cheering us on to resist, at every turn, the death-dealing forces of body injustice. To resist is to choose life.*

Strong-Hearted One, give us courage to resist oppression, whether our own or those around us. Remind us that Love is greater than any injustice.

---

*In the midst of the many body oppressive systems there are always others who are resisting with us. See the appendix for some of these resistance movements who are pushing against the violence of body injustice to liberate the body.

REFLECTION

1. What are the stories of your family's experience with the death-dealing forces of a system of oppression? If you don't have any, ask yourself why not? If you do, identify who exhibited signs of resistance.
2. All domination systems require that we remain afraid to resist. Yet, in confidence and resistance, many songs, especially gospel tunes, have an empowering message that urges us to take heart and push on refusing to give in. What music encourages your active resistance to being dehumanized? If you have none, ask your friends and start a list to sing or listen to when you feel unvalued.
3. In the face of death-dealing systems of oppression, where some bodies are not meant to survive, which faith statements encourage you to "keep on keepin' on"? Start a list of affirmations, biblical verses, quotes, and statements that remind you of the ancestors, this "cloud of witnesses," that cheers us on to resist the inhumanity of the system.

    None of us is immune to the influence of the power of oppression. Who are the people, either as individuals or groups, whom you now or in the past considered to be "less than"? Now write a prayer to wrestle with our ability to be both the oppressor and the oppressed.

When the Body is the Target

MEDITATION

I am sending you out like sheep into the midst of wolves,
so be wise as serpents and innocent as doves.

Matthew 10:16

Society can be cruel. State-sponsored violence is real. We too often yield to the impulse to target certain bodies, allowing or even encouraging all-too-real threats. Whether by bigotry-fueled supremacy, self-righteous arrogance masking insecurity, or systemic evil baked into the political, economic, and social structures, body injustice is a lived reality for too many. Whether the issue is race, gender or gender identity, or sexual orientation, justifications are found to exclude, ridicule, threaten, or attack. How do we respond when targeted or when people or powers decide our bodies are "other," devalued, and expendable? One thing is certain: This is the time to be "as wise as a serpent and harmless as a dove" (Matthew 10:16). Rarely is it wise to go it alone. Fighting oppressive forces requires supportive community.

Through the ages, people have struggled against violence and vilification by others. Elijah did. As a prophet chosen by God to speak truth to corrupt power, he gained the attention and ire of the queen, who vowed to have him killed (1 Kings 19:1–2). How did he survive the threats to his body and well-being? He was as wise as a serpent and ran for safety (1 Kings 19:3), finding someone to help him hide. He relied on God's protection during difficult times (1 Kings 17:15–16). Yet, even as God's protection and intervention continued, Elijah despaired. Feeling alone, he thought he was the only one left (1 Kings 19:4,10).

The message from God was that not only was he not alone, but that two entire communities just like him were also being protected (1 Kings 18:3–4,13). Knowing that others are with us in the struggle against oppression can give us strength and courage, sometimes from unexpected places. For Elijah, his communities were in two separate caves. For us, it might be likeminded friends, individual or unexpected allies, or supportive faith communities.

To be as harmless as doves is to lean into one another for comfort and reassurance of survival. To be as wise as serpents is to do the hard work of strategizing for the survival of all. We can do this, but it will be together.*

One who sees the sparrow, see the bodies that are targeted. See the pain and suffering even as you see and judge the unacceptable injustice of targeting people. We know you protect us; be at our side as we seek justice for all bodies.

REFLECTION

1. Sometimes we feel alone because of misguided expectations. Elijah expected people to be where he was but they were in caves waiting until it was safe. Elijah expected God to be in the fire, wind, or earthquake but found God in the silence (1 Kings 19:11–12). Some translations say "whisper" or "still small voice."

*Seeking liberation from body oppression is difficult; doing that work with professional help may be necessary. I have recommended AASECT certified sexual health professionals in the introduction of this book. See Further Resources for Healing Body Injustice in the Appendix for some of those people and organizations who not only resist body injustice for themselves but are organizing justice-seekers to build a wider community of support for social change.

a. If you were going through a difficult crisis, who would you call? List all those you could count on in difficult times.
b. List the groups of people and organizations who would care if you were having an emergency or hard time.
c. Identify the various physical locations where you might feel safe from danger.

2. Which of the following scriptural affirmations might be helpful in times of trouble?
   a. "Be still and know that I am God." (Psalm 46:10)
   b. "I will never leave you or forsake you." (Hebrews 13:5)
   c. "For I, the LORD your God, hold your right hand; it is I who say to you, 'Do not fear, I will help you.'" (Isaiah 41:13)
   d. "For the kingdom of God depends not on talk but on power." (1 Corinthians 4:20)
   e. ". . . you are from God and have conquered them, for the one who is in you is greater than the one who is in the world." (1 John 4:4)
   f. "'Vengeance is mine. I will repay,' says the Lord." (Romans 12:19)
   g. Add your own. ______________________________

Sexual Justice is Body Justice: Listen and Love

MEDITATION

You do not receive our testimony.

John 3:11

The early church broke societal barriers in favor of enthusiastic equality (Acts 2:44, Galatians 3:28), but years later Christian teaching was codified by teachers driven by their own sexual turmoil and unable to write inclusively or think positively about the joy of sexual pleasure. Their cultural context led them to conform to the patriarchal thinking of the Empire. Empire thinking still reigns today. And we who want to be more sexually liberated must take notice that it is a *white, male, and heterosexual* empire.

The Empire thinking of "the flesh," as the apostle Paul calls it, operates on the principle of *power over*: men over women, straights over gays, rich over poor, white people over people of color, able-bodied over differently abled, and, arrogantly labeled, "first world" over Indigenous cultures and developing countries. Thus, sexuality of "the world" could be irresponsible hedonism driven by the most powerful one in the room. This is evident in the twentieth and twenty-first centuries, when husbands can rape their wives, gay people are thrown into jail, and trans people are put to death. However, Jesus and his immediate followers were countercultural in that they operated out of *power with*. Expressions of sexuality driven by the spirit of *power with* would be boundary-less, inclusively egalitarian, and marked by respect, honesty, and compassion.

Nicodemus recognized Jesus's teaching was different, but he couldn't get it (John 3:7, 10,11). Jesus had a much bigger frame, a wider vision that included the "the least of these," prioritizing love over power, love-in-action, not warm fuzzy feelings. Love takes notice of and responds to the needs of the flesh of one another, whether they be hunger, poverty, incarceration, substandard wages, or the sexualization and marginalization of those whose way of being in the world is different from our own. Jesus tells Nicodemus that his lack of understanding was because he was not hearing the testimony of others. Neither Nicodemus nor we can understand fully unless we hear the testimony of those whose bodies are being treated unjustly (John 3:11). For every white body that has been oppressed, there are bodies of color and Indigenous bodies that have been both sexually and racially oppressed. For every straight white body that is bullied, there are queer and trans bodies of color and indigenous bodies that are violated and oppressed by class, race, gender, and sexuality. This is "intersectionality," the intersections of injustice. And some of us have far more painful intersections than others. Are we listening?

Jesus wanted Nicodemus to think and listen differently, to receive other's testimonies rather than stay in the shadows of his own spiritual ignorance. To hear difficult testimonies about body injustice, however, means we must open ourselves to the pain of another and our own complicity in that pain. No white or heterosexual or cisgender or able-bodied person can be sexually and spiritually free while other bodies are being oppressed. We open the door to bodily justice by listening and lovingly responding to those testimonies different from our own.

Truthteller, hold us accountable to listen, to learn, and to love.
Give us fortitude when the testimony is painful. Give us

patience with our own ignorance. Give us grace to re-examine our hearts. May we see your promises more clearly.

REFLECTION

1. Identify someone unlike yourself and ask yourself if you know their testimony about living in their body?
2. Read a memoir or biography of someone from a very different background, racially, ethnically, or from a different class or world experience. Consider it a sacred revelation, a testimonial gift to you.
3. Empire thinking maintains the status quo of body injustice. In what ways do you disrupt Empire thinking in your life?

part three

Ethics Without Repression?

Think On these Things

You were called to freedom . . .
only do not use your freedom as an
opportunity for self-indulgence.

Galatians 5:14

For some more conservative Christians, the experience of freedom carries with it a level of fear that we may find ourselves moving out of our rationality and into our bodies, incapable somehow of making sound decisions about the most loving thing to do for ourselves and one another. If such an experience of freedom *did* remove sanity, then that fear would be justified. In fact, it does not. To the contrary, there is significant scientific evidence that absorbed repression may lead us to act out in unhealthy or even dangerous ways. Repression is the problem, not freedom. These miraculous bodies of ours are not to be feared but to be accepted as part of the gift of "self-ness" we are given by God; not to be repressed and controlled, but guided.

For people of faith who seek to follow the example of Jesus in making life decisions, or those who wish to become righteous people, it is unlikely we will become hedonistic in the face of sexual freedom. For those who seek to live by biblical standards of righteous living, scripture is clear: a totally self-absorbed hedonist lives in luxury with a fat heart (James 5:5), is swollen with conceit rather than loving God (2 Timothy 3:4), is choked by pleasure so that they cannot engage in righteousness (Luke 8:14), and it is all about ego (James 4:3). None of these biblical passages are condemnations of the sensual life or of sexuality per se. Instead, they all rail against the ego-centered hedonistic priorities that take precedence over spiritual righteousness, understanding righteousness not as keeping religious rules but as actions grounded in love (Romans 8:27,28, Matthew 23:23,27, Micah 6:8). Sexual freedom then does not have to equal irresponsible hedonism, and repression is not a healthy alternative. There is significant room for sexual freedom to exist between these two extremes.

As sexually liberated Christians who find the sacred in and through our bodies' experiences, our spiritual task is to discern how to be responsibly free in our bodies and with the decisions we make. We use the life and teachings of Jesus and the writings of the early Christians, particularly the apostle Paul, even as we keep them in dialogue with how contemporary science understands sexual health and well-being and what constitutes a healthy relationship. We also listen to the internal voice of the Spirit and our lived experience. This process of spiritual discernment moves us away from practices based on obedience and conformity to imposed rules and into a prayerful seeking to know God's will for our lives. This kind of faith rests in humility and self-reflection and relies upon self-understanding that unfolds into maturity and wisdom.

Think on these things as you consider sexual decision-making and how to live in responsible relationship body-to-body.

- How well do you know yourself, both your strengths and your weaknesses?
- Whom do you obey and why?
- Are you comfortable with making your own decisions in life or do you second guess yourself?
- How much control do you give to God? To others? To yourself?
- What part of being sexually free do you find difficult?

I Am Not My Behavior

MEDITATION

I do not understand my own actions.
For I do not do what I want, but I
do the very thing I hate.

Romans 7:15

I often behave in ways that reflect I do not like my body.
But who I really am is a
human body Divinely proclaimed as "very good."
I sometimes act impulsively and stupidly.
But who I really am is a
human learning from mistakes.
I say I believe in God's goodness yet live in fear of God's judgment.
But who I really am is a
spiritual seeker longing for home.
I try to cover my deficiencies, weaknesses, and insecurities.
But who I really am is a
beloved child of God.
I live in my imperfections, guilt-ridden and ashamed.
But who I really am is
abundantly forgiven and covered in grace.
I listen to the false beliefs and lies about my worth from those around me
But who I really am is
held in God's steadfast love.

I appoint myself as the judge and the jury of my behavior.
But who I really am is
only slightly lower than the angels.
I live imprisoned and condemned in this false jail of my
    unworthiness
But who I really am is a
prisoner squatting in a cell with an open door.
Freedom awaits.
Any time now.[20]

One Who Understands, we confess we do not see ourselves as you see us. Forgive us for treating ourselves so poorly, not loving ourselves enough. We confess our distortions mean we cannot hear the good news of your extravagant love and abundant desires for our lives. Remind us, over and over, that this sin of distortion can become the standard we apply to others as well. Help us to accept all of ourselves just as you do. Thank you.

REFLECTION

1. Experiential activity: In the poem above, the first lines of each stanza reflect shame and unworthiness, the parts usually considered to be sinful, while the focus of the next lines speak to a deeper truth. Read them aloud. "Who I really am is . . ." Repeat a second time, but this time assume a pose of confidence.
2. Experiential activity: Stand in front of a mirror and put your hand on your heart as though the hand of God was touching you. Now repeat the second lines as before and with each word, pat your heart in rhythm. Allow yourself to take in the affirming and loving words through this touch on your body.

3. How easy was it to let go of the shame and claim the promise? Identify which line(s) were the most difficult and write down the response(s) to display in places where they can be seen throughout the day.

The Deceitful Ego

MEDITATION

The heart is devious above all else;
it is perverse—who can understand it?

Jeremiah 17:921

When the verse above is applied to sexuality, the speaker may mean: "Do not trust your body, your feelings, or sexual desires or longings." By using this verse to admonish us to distrust our hearts, the implication is that all yearnings of the heart and desires of the flesh are suspect and sinful.

But our hearts, the essence of who we are, the deepest spiritual truth of ourselves, originate from and are in the heart of God. When we are at our best and listen to our deepest selves, our heart longs for goodness for ourselves and others. And, while it is true that we all have the capacity to deceive or harm ourselves and others, if we are made in God's image, then perhaps deceitful hearts are not an inherent flaw but rather our inattention to the voice of God. So, rather than assume deceit and dismiss the possibility of well-intentioned hearts, let's suggest that this scripture is talking about the unrighteous behavior that results from listening to the ego. The ego insists on being better than others, demanding center stage to get all the attention, and having its own way. The ego cannot love others in its self-absorption. It is this self-importance that creates a narcissistic self, unable to see the neighbor or the negative consequences of its self-absorption. The result? Deceitful and unrighteous actions that ultimately damage both ourselves and the community. Jeremiah is not condemning the heart but pointing to the consequences of listening to ego.

As it relates to sexuality and making sexual decisions, then, this passage is suggesting that we ask ourselves a question: Who is in charge? The self-absorbed or narcissistic ego? Or our higher self, the one that resembles God?*

O Seer of the Heart, open our hearts to the goodness that is inside us. Help us recognize when we are listening to our higher self that finds its home in you. Help us resist the labels to which others want us to conform. Instead, may Love be our guiding light and our moral compass. Teach us to listen more closely to what Love would have us do. And may we act on our body's needs, our longings, and desires in a way to promote love for ourselves and for others.

REFLECTION

1. Experiential Activity: Identify a sexual concern or issue that you are struggling with and set up two chairs facing one another: In one sits your ego and in the second is your higher self. Sitting in one chair, state the issue to start a dialogue and then, while sitting in the opposite chair, respond to the statement. Remember your ego wants its own way, while the higher self is at home and in love with itself and with others. See what they say to one another.

*For more on the ego see meditation "The Self-Care Struggle."

2. Repeat aloud:

   My heart is not deceitful. My heart is confused.
   My heart is filled with goodness. And my heart is conflicted.

   My ego wants what it wants. My ego does not rest.
   My ego demands to be heard. My ego protects and harms me.

   My body has wants and needs. My body is acceptable to God.
   My body is bombarded with conflicting needs. My body conveys God's image.

   My heart and my ego make me human. My faith guides them both.
   My faith frees me from my ego. My faith follows my heart.

   Now, identify which lines created comfort or discomfort and journal your reaction.

3. Identify the self-defeating messages that tell you that your body is not to be trusted or that it is sinful. Make a list of these messages. Then read it aloud but follow each by saying, "I am a work in progress. I am accepted and loved just as I am."

Pausing the Discussion of Virginity

MEDITATION

Now concerning virgins,
I have no command of the Lord.

1 Corinthians 7:25

Some Christians treat women's virginity as a prize to be awarded to her husband. Virginity is never taught in medical schools and is neither a physical nor medical condition. Rather, it is a socially defined concept that Jesus never taught.[22] It is a vestige from a time and culture that understood women as property and was a signifier to the "seller"—that is, the bride's father and her brothers—that guaranteed unused merchandise to the "buyer." In the house church of Corinth, the early followers of The Way were confused as social norms were being turned upside down due to the stories of Jesus's teachings about the body and gender. What about the bodies of the Gentiles previously defined as "unclean"? And, if women were not impure or considered as property, then what was the place of women in leadership and, if the realm of God were imminent, then what about marriage? The new converts sent their list of questions to the apostle Paul for advice. While his advice and counsel was from another time and place that may or may not be helpful in our age, what is of interest is that he honors the limitation of his own knowledge. Note the lack of moralistic judgment and his willingness to highlight that his response about virginity was only an opinion. Since it was not from God, he offered the Corinthians, "take it or leave it 'cause it's the best I can do."

An effective leader is one with no grandstanding ego demanding the spotlight. Paul does not elevate himself nor cover his lack of knowledge with a definitive answer. The humility and honesty he modeled toward others' sexual decision-making is instructive. The focus for us is to discern what is best for us. Spiritual discernment is far more important to faith than genitalia.

Giver of good things, thank you for the gift of understanding and forgiving our moralistic and judgmental ways. Remind us to say, "I don't know" to more freely allow the seeking of the Spirit's guidance. Make us perceptive and keep us honest to express our limits.

REFLECTION

1. We tend to make judgments of others' sexual choices or sexuality based on one of two things: It doesn't attract or interest us, possibly repelling us; or it is something we are attracted to but ashamed to admit. Since Jesus did not teach the Ten Commandments of Sexuality but used an ethics of love to determine behavior, we need humility in our choices and in our judgments. Do an internal review and make a list of various aspects of sexuality and sexual behaviors that make you uncomfortable and uneasy or repulse you as unacceptable and/or sinful. Then, using a scale of one through ten with ten as the most judgmental, rate yourself compared to the apostle Paul's lack of judgment. Identify which of these sexual topics are the most problematic for you and ask yourself why this is so.
2. Now read each item on your list aloud but follow each one with the following statements:

"I do not know what is best for others. I am not their judge."

3. Now read each item on your list aloud but follow each one with the following statements:

"I do not know what is best for others. I am not their judge. I do the best I can so neither will I judge myself."

4. Body work (if you are able): Recall all the sexual rules you have heard and as you remember each, feel it in your body as a burdensome yoke. As you read or state each new limitation, feel it accumulate and shift your body into a stooped position. Feel the additional weight of judgment pushing you down.

   From this stooped position, repeat the following phrase as you slowly rise to a standing position:

"I am free to find my own way without others' judgments,
for I am loved.
I am free because my Guide is The Giver of Good Things."

   Now standing, assume a confident posture that reflects this freedom and repeat the phrase again until you feel the freedom of the words within your body.

The Ethical Doorway to Pleasure

MEDITATION

Let your word be "Yes, Yes" or "No, No.

Matthew 5:37

Pleasing: Acquiescence seldom leads to pleasure. Acquiescence is given a positive spin as "pleasing others," but it often necessitates leaving out one's own pleasure; it is not a long-term strategy for either a vibrant spiritual life or healthy relationship. Too often, "pleasing" entails giving up our own moral agency, sometimes to our own detriment. Thus, habitual "pleasing" can easily lead to resentment. Christians often translate pleasing others as being kind, but in our sexual lives, that acquiescence, without full enthusiastic consent, allows the passive breaking of personal boundaries.

Pleasure without Memory: Some depend on alcohol or drugs to avoid feelings of sexual shame. Sexual acquiescence with chemicals bypasses religiously instilled guilt. Supposedly, the excuse of being "wasted" is a lesser and more understandable "sin" than the "sin" of seeking sexual satisfaction. Absolving themselves of personal responsibility, drugs or alcohol can be blamed instead. While this may allow for minimal pleasure, it dulls or erases the memory of it!

Pleasure: Being a pleaser or relying on chemicals will never release sexual potential nor will it open us to true sexual pleasure. A full immersion into consensual pleasure through sexual intimacy requires being sexually confident (power), acting on our own behalf (agency), and conversation (communication).[23] Approaching the pleasure doorway requires that we ask: "Am I in complete control of my own actions (power)? Am I unapologetic about and comfortable with my boundaries, needs, and interests (agency)? And can I speak about this effectively? (communication)" Freed from guilt, shame, and fear, this doorway allows for unapologetic, uninhibited, yet carefully discerned sexual pleasure. This path leads to the intimacy of an embodied pleasure designed by the Creator.

Truthful One, teach us how to be as real and honest as you are with us. Give us the courage to say "No" and mean it and to say "Yes" without apology. Help us distinguish being "nice" and non-confrontative from the experience of being authentic and honest. Show us the doorway toward intimacy that empowers us to freely communicate on our own behalf. May we know intimacy's depths that you desire with us.

REFLECTION

1. Journaling: How hard is it to be true to yourself without apology? We cannot treat our neighbor as we wish to be treated if we do not listen to and honor our own needs and desires first. Identify a time when you acquiesced with a "yes" without fully meaning it. Write out the exchange that you held silently with yourself or that you had with the other without your full assent. Rewrite the exchange but set aside the role of "pleaser" and stay true to yourself. Perhaps it is to say, "I really need . . ." and "What I would like is . . ." How does it feel to advocate for what you want?
2. Not everyone is happy when we choose to become more authentic to our own needs and desires. Some relationships rely on one partner always giving in, sexually or otherwise. Remember a time of acquiescing to another and read out loud the following:

- I am worthy in God's eyes and I am loved without question.
- My needs are as important as everyone else's.
- I am in charge of me, no one else is. I am my own responsibility.
- I am in charge of seeking to meet my needs. It's an act of self-love.
- I am in charge of caring for myself. Self-love is self-care.
- If I don't listen to myself, then how can I hear God speaking?
- If I don't advocate for myself, then how can God use me?

Breaking the Rules

MEDITATION

your lovemaking is sweeter than wine

Song of Songs 1:2 and 7:1224

We have many unwritten rules around sexuality in the United States. Some of the rules are about who can enjoy sexual intimacy, with whom, how many, and under what circumstances. But sometimes people break sexual rules, and there is no better example of this than the couple in the Song of Songs. Here an unmarried heterosexual couple has sex and enjoys every guilt-free and shame-free minute of their time together. In the era when it was composed, women were not presented as morally autonomous or sexually free but as property of the male. However, in this song, there is no apparent power imbalance, no conversations about marriage or marital plans to make it legitimate (regardless of the insertion of the words "bride" and "groom" by the translators), nor is there a suggestion of a dowry negotiation.[25]

The couple's sensual metaphors don't necessarily work for us today. A woman's breasts as clusters on the vine (7:7), her breath as apples (7:8), cheeks like halves of a pomegranate, (4:7) and a neck like the Tower of David, (4:4) would probably not be considered romantic. Yet, these metaphors reflect a deep immersion into the sensuality of their affair. And this glorious celebration of the erotic is in our bible!

Jesus's relationships appear to be egalitarian and affirming of difference while his non-judgmental teachings were guided by love.

So, using his teachings, what sexual and gender rules imposed in our culture or from the church need to be challenged? And yes, keep in mind that Jesus was a rule-breaker.*

God of the heart, you desire transformed hearts and acts of kindness, mercy, and humility, rather than outward obedience to rules. Stay by our side as we learn to live fully sexual lives. Keep us mindful of the pain we can inflict and the consequences of our decision-making about intimacy. Guide our hearts to know the right path, and when we mess up, forgive us.

REFLECTION

1. Imagine you were going to update the Song of Songs and its sexual metaphors into today's vernacular. Describe three body parts with metaphors that focus on smells, touches, tastes, or sounds.
2. Which restrictive sexual rule(s) in our culture do you think has/have created the most guilt or shame? How has this restrictive rule damaged individuals? How has it affected the society at large?
3. What would a sexually free and ethically responsible society look like?

*For a companionable meditation on sexual rules, freedom, and the heart see "Greatly Beloved Were You to Me."

Feelings Are Not Sinful

MEDITATION

There is nothing outside a person
that by going in can defile.
Mark 7:15

If we think of ourselves as sinful sexual creatures rather than images of the Divine, then certain interpretations of scripture may well confirm what we expect: Feelings are bad or sinful, and most especially sexual feelings, desires, and needs. This conclusion suggests the Creator made us with flawed and disturbingly sinful feelings. While some label human sexuality as sinful, a wiser view would be that the body and our sexual feelings and desires are morally neutral. Behaviors and actions can and do have consequences, whether positive or negative (Matthew 7:20).

When Jesus teaches the priority is to love God and our neighbor as ourselves, this is a love ethic that focuses on behavior, not feelings. Biblical love is never relegated to feelings but to actions toward ourselves and others. Jesus's teaching in Matthew calls us to pay attention to feelings, not because they are bad, but because they may lead us to engage in unrighteous behavior. If we become enraged or angry, we may commit murder (Matthew 5:21–22). If we covet what someone else owns, we may try to steal what is not ours (Matthew 5:28). These feelings without actions do not condemn us but can alert us to possible ethical dilemmas. Jesus was clear that it is the actions that come out of us that defile (Mark 7:21–23).

Feelings are part of humanity, and we dare not condemn what the Creator proclaims to be "very good." Rather, we learn the biblical lessons of mindfulness to our inner state as a source of our behavior toward others and ourselves.

Kind God, Loving One, Merciful Goodness, thank you for the range of human emotions that enrich and enliven our lives with others. Forgive us when we have labeled sexual feelings as wrong or unworthy. May we be wise to accept our humanity and the mishmash of all our sensual and sexual feelings. Help us to choose our behaviors appropriately and righteously. Help us embrace our full humanity with all our glorious potential for good.

REFLECTION

1. The character of Hermione in *Harry Potter and the Order of the Phoenix* notes that some people have a range of emotions that would fit into a teaspoon. Make a list of every emotion you can think of and note those you have been expected to hide, limit, or not experience. Note those emotions that might be related to sexual intimacy. What do you notice about the list? Examine the emotions you've highlighted and determine how large a measure you were allowed to have. Is it more than a teaspoon?
2. Experiential activity: Showing emotion requires vulnerability, particularly those feelings we are told not to express. Which emotion do you find most difficult to express? Move your body into a position that best expresses this emotion. Hold for five seconds and return to a resting position. Then move into a different posture to express that same emotion. Hold for five seconds. Repeat a third time. Journal your relationship to this particular feeling. Can we accept that all emotions are neutral?

The Self-Care Struggle

MEDITATION

I do not understand my own actions.
For I do not do what I want, but I do
the very thing I hate.

Romans 7:15

To the house church in Rome the apostle Paul shared his struggles between his fleshly self and his life in the spirit, despairing at his inability to be his higher self. His fleshly self does not mean he was obsessed about sex or his sexual desires. Rather, for him, 'flesh' is shorthand for those impulses that are diametrically opposed to the life of the Spirit. Paul refers to this fleshly self as 'the old self' (Colossians 3:9, Romans 6:6) that has now been replaced by a 'new self' with a different set of priorities of the Spirit. Unfortunately, the 'old self' that has been shaped by those impulses wants control to ensure its own needs are met first and foremost.

So while the 'old self' that listens to the world's standards wants to be center stage for the applause, it does not care whether or not we make wise choices. It is not our spiritual friend. It wants what it wants, now, at whatever the cost. It does not want to be righteous or loving and it certainly does not want to be Spirit-led. It is singularly uninterested in engaging in a healthy practice of self-care unless it gains admirers or power. It would never admit that our bodies need gentle and loving attention or that our spirits need quiet rest and peaceful silence. It is a paradox. For it is only by loving and caring for ourselves, mind, body and spirit, the very thing that our 'old self' ignores, that we find our spiritual center.

Rescuer God, save us from disregarding our emotional and sexual needs and desires or those of others. Teach us to love ourselves as you love us. Teach us to care for these vessels of flesh and spirit. As we return to your love may we care for ourselves more.

For more about this topic see "The Deceitful Ego."

REFLECTION

1. In your journal make lists of the ways in which you care for your body, mind, and spirit. Is your self-care equally balanced or off-balance? Do you work harder on one than the other? If so, why?
2. Staying busy and caring for others may distract us from the needs and desires of our spirits and bodies. Remember God often speaks in a "still, small voice" (1 Kings 19:12) so our self-care can create sacred space and time as well. Your assignment today is to open yourself to an experience of beauty and/or compassion. Listen and watch for the touch and intervention of the Divine.
3. Choose a self-care task to do today that feels right and then do it!

Sometimes You Do What Ya Gotta Do (To Survive)

MEDITATION

Then she got up and went away,
and taking off her veil she put on the
garments of her widowhood.

Genesis 38:19

The biblical story of Tamar (Genesis 38) cannot be summarized tritely as, "when life gives you lemons, make lemonade." It is about death, betrayal, poverty, and survival for Hebrew widows with no means of supporting themselves. As a widow, Tamar's survival meant that the only security for her old age depended on male offspring. Since her deceased husband couldn't provide this, his brother was required by religious law to do so. When his brother didn't care about her survival, then her father-in-law was responsible. Yet, he wouldn't either. She was stuck. The system, such as it was, failed her. From her community she received only spying and gossiping, not assistance. End of the road. Starve, Tamar.

Tamar was on her own. Sink or swim. Starve or survive. She chose the latter. Modern readers would prefer she had a better social safety net, or a community that welcomed her, or legal representation to hold her father-in-law accountable. But none was available, so she conceived of an unorthodox plan to trap the one who had dismissed her rights. She survived by selling sex to her father-in-law who had reneged on social and familial responsibility. Through secrecy and manipulation, she became the trickster, one whose role is to undermine authority. And undermine she did—the norms of the community, of sexual propriety, and of the family. Sometimes, to survive, ya do what ya gotta do. Tamar used her wits and did so successfully. Our lesson to be learned: We dare not judge those in whose shoes we have never walked.

God of justice, your eyes are on the smallest sparrow, you count the hairs on our head, and do not abandon or forsake us, yet, we fail to create loving ways to care for those in need. Teach us to advocate for justice and provide for those in despair and desperation. Help us lay aside our judgment as others manage unmanageable circumstances. May we lovingly support each other's survival.

REFLECTION

1. How Tamar chose to survive may not be what we would do or want others to do, yet judgment of others' choices is not ours to make. In the following scenarios, rate yourself on a judgment scale of one to ten (one= I'm cool / ten= "May they burn in hell!")
    a. Those who do consensual sex work to determine their own working hours for a decent wage. _______
    b. Those who do consensual sex work as a well-paying service that provides comfort to lonely and needy clients. _______
    c. Those students who do consensual sex work as the best way to pay for college or to pay down the accumulation of school loan debt. _______
    d. Those who do consensual sex work because they can't afford to live on the minimum wage jobs that are available in their city. _______

e. Those homeless minors who turn to sex work after being kicked out of their family home because they identify as gay, trans, or gender fluid. ______

2. Sometimes our loudest judge is an internalization of an angry, judgmental God who punishes, especially sexual issues. Identify one instance that you have experienced as shameful or where you feel judged. Envision a compassionate, accepting God speaking these phrases. Read them aloud, pausing to take them into your heart as truth.

- No one who matters expects perfection from you. Do not expect perfection of yourself. (pause)
- Life is full of choices. Some we make well, some not so well, and some, in hindsight, were mistakes. Let it be. Make amends where necessary. Now move on. (pause)
- Ignore judgment, for Love does not judge, but only guides as it is invited.
- You will survive all manner of hardship, trials, and mistakes. Your life path is your own. Keep walking. Do the best you can.
- Shame cannot survive an outpouring of love. Find love around you. Find love inside you. You will heal.
- You are not fully formed but a work in progress. Your job is to learn. You will grow. All will be well.

The Signs of Self-Love

MEDITATION

Little children, let us love, not in word or speech, but in deed and truth.

1 John 3:18

We don't expect people simply to say they love us. In fact, if a lover does not show outward signs of their love, they will rather rapidly discover they have no relationship! We expect love to be physically expressed, with lovers (and parents and friends) asking, "What would they want me to give them or do with or for them?" By putting ourselves in the other's shoes we answer the question and then show our love, not just "in word or speech, but in truth and in action." Yet, if we are to use the standard for self-love, loving action may get more difficult. How do we show our love for ourselves in truth and in action? What are the marks of those who love themselves? How do they put themselves first? Is self-care part of our daily routine? Can we draw boundaries clearly and hold the line when the needs of others may threaten our own self-loving actions? And, in sexual interactions, is self-love evident in the ability to name what we want and don't want sexually? Can we ask? Do we ask? Or does the partner always take precedent? Frankly, many Christians would flunk the self-love test. Self-love is a often last priority for people habituated not to ask for what we want, especially if it might be in conflict with the needs and desires of others. This message is especially potent for women, but it traps others as well if society has deemed your body differently abled, non-white, carrying the stigma of an immigrant status, or poor and unacceptable.

Whatever the situation, a difficulty in loving ourselves may reflect that we can't accept God's love for ourselves. Can we allow ourselves that much love? If not, we may find ourselves waiting for others to love us instead of taking the responsibility for opening to an acceptance of ourselves and our place in God's love. That waiting for external acceptance is not loving "in truth or in action." God's desire is the ability to stand in our own truth of who we are and what we desire and then to act in loving, accepting, and respectful ways toward ourselves as we do with others.*

Lover God, your love without conditions is overwhelming and too much to take in. Give us a vision of what it means to engage in self-love. Give us the courage to believe we are worth it. Help us see when we treat ourselves badly and then make excuses for withholding self-love. Thank you for hanging in there on this one. Keep reminding us to love so that it can spill out to others. Thanks.

REFLECTION

1. Identify three fun things you could do just for you that feel as if you are spoiling yourself ridiculously. With a pen or pencil in your dominant hand, write one of these desires as you would in a conversation with a caring but firm "inner parent." With your non-dominant hand, write out their response. Continue with the dialogue as new insights about yourself emerge.
2. What pairing of words and actions of love speak most strongly to you? Write down the pairs and read them aloud, noting with each, "I deserve to be loved and accepted as I am."

---

*For an elaboration of why self-love is difficult for some people of faith see meditation, "Finding Joy without J.O.Y."

3. Now identify someone who has been good at expressing in both word and deed their feelings for you. Identify a way you can express your gratitude, in both word and deed.
4. Identify someone to whom you are most likely to verbalize your love. Now ask yourself how you show it to them in deed. If you come up wanting, decide what you can do that would reveal the extent of your feelings. Be sure to choose something that will speak deeply to them. These might include acts of service and helping, giving time or tangible gifts, words of affirmation or touch.[26] The question is what actions would *they* appreciate? Make a plan to follow through.

The Ethics of the Apostle Paul: Freedom

MEDITATION

If you are led by the Spirit,
you are not subject to the law.

Galatians 5:18

In the first century, the Jewish followers of Jesus grappled with various aspects of their faith. Their new insights from Jesus's teaching were sometimes in conflict with earlier religious teachings. For example, were the followers of The Way bound by the rules about eating the food that had been offered to idols? Although the apostle Paul had been a zealous and esteemed Jewish teacher, now he taught that all religious rules are seen through the lens of the spirit of Christ and not through obedience alone. For Paul, it was not because the law was in error but that it was insufficient.

Even as he believed in a freedom from man-made rules and restrictions, Paul understood Christians to be bound by an ethic of love. We are to listen to the Spirit even as we live into our freedom. To apply this freedom to sexuality, Paul could easily be saying that sexual freedom is a given. Yet, our freedom cannot be used in such a way to create difficulties for someone else.

Thus, all things are allowed even as not all things are beneficial (1 Corinthians 12:23). We are free to discern what is the most loving thing in each situation. For example, what will bring joy and what behaviors might have negative consequences? Whose voice are we listening to? Are we trying to stay obedient to others' rules? Are we trying to stretch rule-following in such a way to prop up an illusion of obedience to a standard we don't want to keep? Does a decision that is grounded in my freedom feel as if it has integrity?

Obviously then, the context of our sexual freedom, lived with integrity as we discern what makes our own sex life ethical and acceptable to God, will require a maturity in self-awareness, an honesty about our motives, and a consideration of the other person(s) involved and possible consequences. It cannot be a hormonally driven justification for irresponsible hedonism. When we live in the abundant love of God, our minds and hearts will engage in righteous living.

Freedom-loving God, we know that love will not box us into restrictions that limit joy and pleasure. Yet we are afraid of our freedom and sometimes prefer to hide rather than choose life. Give us courage to live into your love more fully and freely and keep us from all fear.

REFLECTION

1. A thought experiment: Knowing you have the freedom in the name of God's love to engage in our deepest desires, think of

the wildest never-to-be-believed sexual fantasy that you might have and then apply Paul's ethical principles.

   a. Can you relish this kind of freedom in your imagination? What does it feel like to know this freedom would not incur God's wrath but perhaps even prompt God's pleasure? How comfortable are you with your own sexual freedom?
   b. If you had the opportunity, could you live out the fantasy without guilt or shame? Would there be regrets? If you acted on this permission, would you like yourself in the morning? Would you feel guilt-ridden if you lived into your freedom?
   c. What consequences might there be for others who joined you? Or within the wider community if it became known? Can you anticipate any physical, emotional, or spiritual harm in this activity? How might you think about this behavior in terms of freedom but also responsibility?

2. Body Movement: Use your body posture to illustrate the following:
   a. "All things are (sexually) permissible" (first posture)
   b. "but not all things are (spiritually) beneficial" (second posture)
   c. Repeat three more times and note if your postures convey shame or guilt. If so, choose new postures that do not.

The Ethics of the Apostle Paul: The Conscience

MEDITATION

All things are permitted, but not all things are beneficial. All things are permitted, but not all things build up.

1 Corinthians 10:23

The apostle Paul taught the house church in Corinth that their freedom was grounded in the life of the Spirit, but that freedom cannot be used in ways that create difficulties for one's own or another's conscience. So, while all things are allowed, not all things are beneficial to be acted upon (10:23). Complete freedom is always bound by the constraints of love. In sexual decisions, if our conscience tells us we are not being honest with ourselves or with a potential partner or if we feel uneasy or guilt-ridden, then the priority must be to listen to that inner voice before proceeding. Only a free conscience will allow us to enjoy deeply the moment and the experience. But it goes further.

We must also ask ourselves if our choices have the potential to lead others astray (1 Corinthians 8:10–13). In the name of loving one another, we are not to become a "stumbling block" for others (1 Corinthians 8:9). Since we can never fully know others' minds, this is difficult to discern. Yet, this important ethical caution suggests it is never only about ourselves, but that we must seek to choose what is best for others as well. We may not cause harm, and it is always better to err on the side of self-denial of personal freedom if the alternative might be to create pain or suffering, guilt, or shame for others (1 Corinthians 8:13).[27]

This kind of ethic requires that we ask, "Am I being honest with myself and my partner?" "Have we considered our intentions and consequences carefully?" It also requires a deeper assessment of the needs and desires of the one with whom we are contemplating a possible sexual interaction and the adequate communication skills and understanding to assure there is full consent. For Christians, sexual behaviors can never be a hormonally driven justification or acquiescence, especially if this could lead to harm. Ethical and moral sexual decision-making always results in behaviors that include both self-love and self-care and respectful, honest, and open communication with potential partners. Monitoring one's conscience and clarifying the moral standards of the other requires that we listen deeply before moving into our freedom.

God of our conflicted minds and hearts, sometimes we are confused by what our bodies want and the rules of what we should or should not do. Sometimes in our confusion there are too many options or too few. We hear conflicting voices. Minds and hearts are in tension and conflict. Life is complicated. Remind us of one simple rule: to love both ourselves and others. Quiet us to listen more carefully.

REFLECTION

1. Examine your conscience to see if you can identify any sexual actions for which you feel guilt.
   a. In order to live in peace with a guilty conscience we often justify and rationalize. If you have done so, be aware of it and let yourself feel the regret.

b. Is there is a way to make amends with another person?

c. Give thanks for your conscience for the noisy reminders of our errors in judgment, hurtful actions, and misdoings.

d. Remembering there are no standards of perfection and that divine forgiveness is always at hand, what would it take to release yourself from the cover of rationalizations? How can you ease your conscience before God or others?

2. Find two spaces about twelve feet apart. Decide on one ethical dilemma you are considering in your life and state it out loud. Slowly walk to the point farthest from you and state your case for why you should take one particular action. Then physically move to the second point and give the reasons why that is not a good idea. Repeat as needed. Listen to the equally valid reasons at both ends.

   a. Next, use the two points to ask, "What is the most loving action for me?" and "What is the most loving action for others?" The goal is to explore the complexities and the nuance.

If walking is difficult or space is limited, do this exercise mentally or on paper.

We Just Wanna Have Fun

MEDITATION

We played the flute for you, and you did not dance.

Matthew 11:17

There are a range of motivations for seeking physical intimacy: the desire to be touched, held, and caressed, the physical release of tension, the search for comfort or affirmation, to be "seen" and acknowledged, and to express and intimately share love with one's beloved. While there are undoubtedly others, the one most troublesome for many to admit is that sometimes we simply want to have some fun. This is a perfectly human desire. Why not have pleasure? Play with abandon? Relax in a state of shared bliss? Momentarily lay aside worries, stresses, or cares to experience the joy and delight that our physical bodies can bring, especially when shared with another.

If sexy pleasure is difficult to consider, then ask yourself, "How playful is my God?" If not at all, re-examine your conclusion. Where does this somber image come from? What purpose does it serve? What would happen if we were to envision a God who laughs when we laugh and who takes great delight in our pleasure, including in the bedroom?

Jesus did not share such a restrictive image of God. His leadership did not include sitting on the sidelines of life and pontificating in all seriousness. Rather, Jesus attended feasts and banquets. He was called "a glutton and a drunkard" (Matthew 11:19) by those who may have heard the music of life but did not dance to it. If Jesus is our model, then we dance for the joy and pleasure that all of life brings.

Maker of good feelings and pleasurable bodies, forgive us when we deny our delicious feelings rather than celebrating them. Forgive us when we stop our ears from hearing the call to move our sensual bodies, to dance with the joy and delight that is our birthright. Thank you for those who enjoy life with us. We are grateful for the wonder of our bodies and the depth of the experiences they provide. May it be that in our abandonment to pleasure we see you better as the Creator of such goodness. Thank you.

REFLECTION

1. Choose a pleasurable activity that would give you sensual pleasure and do it, without guilt or shame.
2. What would change in your life if the mantra you heard every day was: *You may not work today until after you have played.*

   Now imagine God saying that to you every morning upon waking. Imagine Jesus saying that to you. Journal a conversation about this new directive for your life.
3. Find your favorite piece of music, get off your chair, and, as you listen or sing along, move your body without guilt or shame. As you dance, focus on the pleasure of your body's movement until you begin to feel a shift that uplifts your spirit.
4. Touch the following body parts as you slowly make these statements aloud:

   (hand on your heart) "We have beautifully made bodies that deserve pleasure."

   (hand on your cheeks) "We each have a sweetness that we dare not forget."

   (hand on your abdomen) "We know the truth of the goodness of life."

(hand on your forehead) "We forget to be good to ourselves."
(hand on your crotch) "We deserve pleasure because pleasure is a gift."

Now repeat and say each statement but change the words to be in first person as "I."

Forgetting the Past

MEDITATION

Do not remember the former things
or consider the things of old.
I am about to do a new thing.

Isaiah 43:18–19a

Most of us carry some guilt and even shame for past sexual decisions we made or didn't make or those that were made for us.

Most of us have made mistakes—and some disasters—even as some were thrust upon us by others. Sometimes we are not aware until long after the fact that we have hurt others or have committed grave offenses. Our sexual issues, whether indiscretions and poor choices or trauma-based, are amplified in a culture that so easily shames sexuality even as it glorifies sexual objectification. Sexual ignorance, power imbalances, and the fact that few of us are prepared to communicate effectively in order to give full consent all create problems. They leave us with bad memories and regrets and oftentimes with scars. What do we do about our own shame and guilt?

Let's recognize we are not alone. Even the apostle Paul acknowledged his own difficulties (2 Corinthians 12:7) and his failure to meet his own expectations as a person of faith (Romans 7:15–20). Contrary to what some teach however, our difficulties relating to sexuality do *not* make them bigger sins! After the Hebrews had been through much difficulty making poor choices, God told them not to live in the past but to leave that all behind. While repair may be a possibility, ultimately, the past cannot be changed. It is not helpful to carry yesterday's weight of unresolved sexual scars and bad memories into our experience of today. Instead, we forgive ourselves for being human even as we forgive others for the same and move on. That work of forgiveness and turning to look forward may require the help of a trained professional; this is a good step, too. The Divine sees our pains and scars and understands our mistakes. We all have them. It is part of the reality of life. Yet, our Still-Creating God cannot make us who we are to be today if we are still living in the past. Each new day God is about to make a new thing. Can we see it?

Giver of each new day, keep reminding us not to carry yesterday's load but to put it into your hands instead. May we forgive ourselves as you always forgive us. Help us to breathe in each precious moment without returning to the past. Keep us focused on what and who is around us in this wondrous world. Remind us of your Presence at the Beginning and the End. Even as you are in the Past and in our Future so we know you through today, the here-and-now. What new thing will you reveal today?

REFLECTION

1. Thought experiment: The apostle Paul spoke about a difficulty as a thorn that was in his side (2 Corinthians 12:7). As a thought experiment, imagine a group of people moving together in a crowd and envision each one with one or more

thorns in their bodies. They move through life always a bit uncomfortable, always a bit in pain, afraid to complain too loudly because it is only a little thorn. What expressions are on their faces? How do they walk? Do they talk to one another? What are the tones of their voices? Now imagine that you can see each thorn and know how to respond for the healing of that wound. In your mind's eye approach, each one and say the following:

"The thorn will come out as you pay attention.
The pain is embedded in your past—not in today.
Wake up to today."

2. Return to the thought experiment and imagine that the power of these words brings surprise and comfort. How does their walking change in the moment? What do they notice around them as they pay attention to "today"? What changes do they experience?
3. Imagine you awoke this morning with a completely empty calendar by your bedside—everything in the past forgiven and all understood and gracefully accepted today. What would be your first act of celebration? What would you do with your new day?

On Being a Sexual Prodigal

MEDITATION

The younger son . . . traveled to a distant region, and there he squandered his wealth in dissolute living.

Luke 15:13

There are some who connect Jesus's parable of the prodigal son to sexuality, suggesting that the "dissolute living" included seeing prostitutes. But while youthful exuberance—sexual or otherwise—can be ill-advised, there are many legitimate reasons to go far from home to seek adventure, satisfy curiosity, or to connect with new people. It is a mark of learning to be independent. Sexual exploration is often a part of this learning.

The King James Version translates his dissolute living as "riotous living." That would usually mean it was an immoderate, rambunctious, or out-of-control lifestyle, one that is not guided by wisdom. Such an understanding would come from the perspective of maturity or perhaps the wisdom of a parent. For the rest of us who are inexperienced, oftentimes we don't know our priorities are messed up until after the fact, which is what the story reveals.

Whatever the son's behavior, sexual or otherwise, the focus of this story is not on what he foolishly or incautiously did, but rather on the astonishing fact that his father didn't wait to hear what he had to say when he returned home. There was no need to hear a confession because the focus was on the joy of the homecoming and the celebration that followed. The story reminds us that we do the best we can (some of it, in hindsight, misguided or stupid), yet we are always greeted by Love when we come to our senses—and, even when we do not. It doesn't matter if the behavior of wild, riotous living is of a sexual nature or not. The important thing is to come to our senses and return to where we are loved.

Seer of All, so here is the deal; sometimes we know what we are doing, or we think we do, and sometimes we are clueless and only figure it out after it all ends badly. We can be a mess, especially about sexuality, but, of course, you already know that. Thank you for the message that you still wait patiently and lovingly for us to come to our senses. Keep calling us. Keep being there. We'll keep trying to find our way back to you.

REFLECTION

1. Think of a time in which you made a sexual mistake that you regret. There's no need for embarrassment since we all make them, but remember the pain of it and the struggle. Now as a wise and caring parent, write a letter to that younger self. What words do you need to hear that would bring comfort? Like the parent in the story, welcome them to their homecoming. Sign your letter with a signature of the Divine.
2. Body movement: Stand before a mirror with your arms wide open at chest level and say, "Welcome home. I've been waiting for you." Now move your arms into a prayer pose and say, "Sometimes I am foolish (or stupid, dumb, or whatever your sense of yourself was at the time you now regret) and I find it hard to forgive myself." Now, open your arms wide again and repeat, "Welcome home. I've been waiting for you." Continue having a conversation between the repentant

side of your humanity and the forgiving side of divinity using these body poses until you feel a resolution.

3. Imagine you are a parent whose offspring is ready to leave the nest. Even as you know they are still immature in some ways, what can you say or do that would give them permission while at the same time reassuring them of your continuing love and support?

The Body as Personal and Private Property

MEDITATION

Your body is a temple of the Holy Spirit within you, which you have from God.

1 Corinthians 6:19

We are each gifted with marvelous bodies designed for the pleasures of living. Each one is perfectly designed by the Creator with a unique personality and with the capacity to contribute toward a more just and loving human community. Thus, each body is the temple where the Holy Spirit resides. As we grow and change, we care for these temples as we are able, understanding that while our body is the gift, the Creator is the Giver. Some of us may be taught that agency over our bodies is not our own; that these temples of the Spirit actually belong to someone else and must be given away.

This harmful idea insists we give power over our bodies to a spouse, in part to serve their sexual needs rather than our own. This gendered and heterosexual idea often privileges male sexual desire over female: the female gives and the male takes. It is unjust to suggest that half the human family is expected to give up ownership of their temple while the other half is entitled to it. Sexual needs do not adhere to a male/female hierarchy, nor do the temples of our bodies need to become the property of another.

If sexual joy is absent, it may be because we have given away ownership of our temple with the Spirit inside. A marriage license does not change nor can it contradict this spiritual truth: the spiritual temple of our physical bodies is personal and private property.

Wisdom Within, forgive us if we are tempted to give up ownership of our lives and bodies to others. While our wisdom about our bodies unfolds, help us love and care for ourselves as the sacred temple where Wisdom resides. Help us love and care for our bodies as a grand temple.

REFLECTION

1. Those who are socialized to be female are often encouraged to give up ownership of various pieces of ourselves. Sometimes this is tangible: the first place in line, the last dip of ice cream, or an hour of time that was to have been for ourselves. Sometimes this causes resentment out of an (unspoken) preference to keep those pieces for ourselves, but at other times, there is a coating of glossy self-congratulations for being good girls, loving wives, or compassionate Christians. This social conditioning in self-sacrifice can be to our own detriment. Whatever your gender identity, make a list of ways you may have given away some piece of yourself this week. Then note those times and ways you were listening to someone else's voice rather than to your own need or preferences.

2. Pretend there is a guilt-o-meter of one through a hundred that measures the extent of your guilt when claiming your own needs and desires (one is to have no guilt and one hundred is to acknowledge you are drowning in it). What number would it register in your guilt
   a. About owning your sexual needs?
   b. Requesting personal time or space?
   c. Resisting the influence of others?
3. Have you ever said "yes" to a sexual activity that you didn't want to participate in? What reason(s) did you give to yourself as a justification? Was it worth it? How will you avoid being dishonest with yourself the next time you are so tempted?

Thinking of Jealousy

MEDITATION

Since there is jealousy and quarreling
among you, are you not fleshly?

1 Corinthians 3:3

Because we are told jealousy is a sign of love, we accept that jealousy is inevitable in every loving relationship. To justify romantic jealousy in the name of love, we cling to the illusion that we can somehow own or control others, supposedly keeping ourselves emotionally safe. Unsurprisingly, this assumption means that jealousy can be used to justify emotional manipulation, abuse, or physical violence. Ultimately, jealousy can be dangerous for our intimate relationships.[28]

In fact, jealousy is never about love but insecurity—we fear losing our partner or being abandoned or replaced. The cycle goes like this: Insecurity leads to a dependence on reassurance that leads to a sense of ownership that leads to guarding with jealousy. If our insecurities remain unchallenged and we believe only this partner can fulfill us or care for us, we may never leave a dysfunctional or abusive relationship.[29]

Messages that feed our insecurities or lack of self-worth do not come from the life or teachings of Jesus. The apostle Paul says that it is only those who are "mere humans" who get stuck in jealousy and quarreling, not followers of the Christ (1 Corinthians 3:3). Our faith allows the noble recognition of our worth as a child of God, leading to mutual respect in relationship.

Christians believe our security and self-worth are found in our Protector, not in our partner. Centering our own well-being in this faith promise means we can avoid the insecurity of jealousy. Our Protector sees us through the eyes of love, saying we are sufficient and beautiful in our own right, with or without our partner. Our Protector is universal and constant Love that says we are worthy of being loved in respectful ways. With this realization we can free our loved ones. They do not belong to us nor we to them. We belong to God.

Protective One, remind us of our value in your eyes so we will turn away from any who treats us otherwise. Give us the wisdom to know which relationships undermine our sense of self-worth and the strength to give up the idolatrous notion we can own or possess another. Help us lay aside all jealousy to focus instead on our own value through your eyes.

REFLECTION

1. If jealousy is an issue in a current romantic relationship, make a list of the ways you are reassured your partner can be trusted. What do they do with you or for you that reflects their commitment to love, honor, and respect you?
2. Examine your own confidence level.
   a. Think of ten reasons why you are a great partner. Do not use external factors like "I am financially secure" or "I'm good looking." Look deeper at your personality, philosophy of life, and values. Read your list aloud, following each item with the statement, "That is a gift I bring to my relationships."
   b. If this is difficult, ask a trusted friend to help make your list. If accepting their observations is difficult, ask yourself why this is so.
   c. If you have a partner and you are willing, ask them what characteristics they appreciate the most in you.
3. Find a body posture that makes you feel confident. Stand in front of the mirror and think of one small fear that provokes jealousy. Does that thought influence your posture? Moving muscles is a way of moving feelings, so shift back into your confident pose. If the posture doesn't help you feel less jealous (this may include anxiety, fear, resentment, anger), then reread the lists you made above and return to the confident posture.
4. If jealousy is a problem in your relationship, seek out a qualified counselor or therapist for some tips on how to address it.

How To Be Sexually Confident

MEDITATION

. . . rightly do they love you.

Song of Songs 1:4

For most of us, there comes a time when we design an idealized intimate partner. We may wish for someone at this particular stage of life or seek a partner for the rest of our lives. The reasons may be emotional, spiritual, physical, or a mix of all three. Finding that "special someone" then becomes a goal. The world, of course, provides answers for attracting a mate that focus on the external: the right body size and shape, wearing the latest fashions, exhibiting symbols of wealth or success, or developing a seductive public persona. But Christians are supposed to focus on the internal. Jesus taught that the standard we use to love others is based on how much we love ourselves (Matthew 22:39). To be most attractive is to have the confidence of one's own self-worth that comes from loving ourselves. This does not mean being "puffed up with conceit" (1 Timothy 3:6), but rather confidently fitting into our own skin. Do we like ourselves? Can we accept ourselves without listening to or using the world's judgments? Can we hold in tension both self-confidence and humility? Can we accept that we have both imperfections as well as unique gifts?

When we are comfortable and confident in loving ourselves, we are our own best company. This removes all sense of desperation in a search for a partner. And because we remain curious about what and where God is leading us and who we will meet along the way, we are not presenting a "needy" persona.

After praying for a companion, one woman heard God respond, "I got this, but it's not time yet." With this assurance she was confident she could lay aside all compulsive searching and simply be open. Without preening or pretense, she could focus on loving herself and being present and open to others. And yes, the prayer was answered, in God's own time.

God-who-has-our-backs, help us be true to ourselves and our desires without being dependent and desperate. Help us focus on loving ourselves and respecting our worth rather than on our needs or our fragility. We trust that when we open our eyes to see ourselves the way you see us, we will become the kind of generous and compassionate people who are attractive to others.

REFLECTION

1. Remember that there is no one else on the planet like you. In your journal, list ten things about yourself that are your gifts to the world. Focus on who you are rather than what you might do. Begin with this sentence, "What I like about myself is that I am . . ." (This may be a difficult exercise, especially if you have been criticized often or exposed to much shame and guilt. Take your time but keep trying.)
2. God is not in the matchmaking business. Our focus on Sacred Love flowing abundantly both toward us and through us, however, will connect us to a confidence that there is sufficient love for all. This kind of loving of self and others, in ways that are not performative but natural, can be attractive. The assignment today is to start a new spiritual discipline of performing one random act of kindness every day. The objective is not to

attract attention or create visibility but to facilitate our own transformation. And over time, we will become more attractive to others.

In Times of Relationship Famine

MEDITATION

In the days of famine they have abundance.

Psalm 37:19

When relationships end, whether by mutual agreement and without recrimination or with hurt feelings and wounds, there may be regret over lost dreams and broken promises, grief, or pain of an uncertain future. With support, one can work through the grief, face the losses, and begin to adjust, readjust, and face the future. Yet, the human spirit needs connection and intimacy and the body longs to be touched, held, and valued. Biology kicks in. Sexual frustration grows. What does one do in a relational and sexual "famine"?

The secular world offers the idea of "friends with benefits," those intimate friendships that assume a physically intimate dimension but with clarity about boundaries. The friendship is the priority, not long-term life commitment or exclusivity. A discussion prior to entering such a relationship may include agreements about boundaries, expectations, permission for personal freedom to grow and change and, when the time is right, to find a new partner. When we are in a famine period devoid of intimacy, can we live moral lives in such relationships? If the definition of morality is mutually exclusive contracts, the answer is no. Yet God is not interested in outward shows of obedience to rules of respectability, nor is there a divine focus on outward gestures (Isaiah 1:11–13, Amos 5: 21,22, Matthew 23:23). Rather, God always looks into the heart (1 Samuel 16:7, Romans 2:29). And fortunately, the psalmist reassures us that, even in times of famine, we will have abundance (37:19).

> *Giver of All Good Things, we confess that we don't like lonely times. We like to be reminded that we are valued and cared for. We admit sometimes we don't like life's timetable and how relationships come and go, leaving us feeling isolated, even if a break-up was for the best. Help us to be patient during times of scarcity. Keep us from being foolish in our choices. Keep our hearts focused on kindness, respect, and honesty so that we will treat others as we wish to be treated.*

REFLECTION

1. Entering a new, significant relationship while still grieving the loss of a previous one can be problematic. Grief prevents us from thinking clearly about our needs. Sometimes a sense of desperation clouds our ability to make wise decisions. It is important, then, to be clear with new relationship partners that this is a time of transition and change. Write in your journal how you might make that clear to someone new.
2. Body movement: Move into a body position that conveys how it feels for you to be alone and grieving the loss of a relationship. After you've found that position, move into a second position that conveys the recollection that you are loved and cared for and not forgotten by an Abundant God. Alternate the two postures while saying the following:
   a. "This is difficult. I know that with time this will pass." (Body position #1)

b. "I am not alone. There are others waiting to help me through." (Body position #2)

3. Because eating might be a distraction to the discomfort of introspection during a time of relationship famine, some people of faith practice fasting to gain clarity for an inner journey. If there are no health consequences, consider setting aside a period of time to fast from solid foods, spending that time thinking about yourself and your needs. Throughout the fast, consider the questions that you might need to seek answers for before beginning another relationship. As you break the fast, say:

   At the first bite say, "This is the day that God has made and it is good." (Psalm 118:24)

   At the second bite say, "I am grateful that I am not forsaken. This is the day that is made by God." (Psalm 9:10)

   At the third bite, say, "I shall be still and listen to the still, small voice." (I Kings 19:12)

   Repeat with each bite. Then review the questions that you plan to answer before entering into a new relationship.

Grieving the Loss of Pleasure in the Purity Culture

MEDITATION

Weeping may linger for the night,
but joy comes with the morning.

Psalm 30:5

Many of us believed the mandate of the purity culture to defer pleasure or we honored the sanctity of an abstinence-only-until-married rule, although the practice is not one Jesus ever taught. We may be upset that those we trusted taught us otherwise. How could we have not seen this? Yet after the anger may come grief. We may grieve decisions made for all the wrong reasons. We may grieve the loss of relationships or the potential for happiness we denied ourselves, the absolute certainty we had depended on, or the reassurance we had of being on the right path. We expected long-delayed intimacy to miraculously appear without baggage. We thought denial of our longings for touch and caress, for connection and mutual love, would someday transform with tenfold power. It seldom does. Anger, pain, grief at loss. All these feelings are real. They are valid. And they will pass in their own time. One day as we move through the pain and grief to our authentic center, we will find that, at our core, there is Love. And pleasure will be waiting for us there.

Ever-Present One in the Valley, sometimes we are too angry to feel you near. Our pain is so deep that we push away comfort even as grief overwhelms. Be here, in all our anger, pain, and grief. In this valley, we feel separated from joy and comfort.

There is no mountain top promise of good times, delight, and pleasure. Be here. Indeed, when all we see or feel is the deep place in the night remind us that joy comes in the morning.

REFLECTION

1. Identify the people who believe in you, who have been there when you needed them. Identify the unexpected encounters or conversations that conveyed the right words or timely insights that you needed. Now choose one of those persons and send a note to convey your gratitude.
2. A thought experiment: The Cave of Sorrow

   If you are grieving a loss of a dream, a relationship, or the regret of time passing or missed opportunities, close your eyes and imagine yourself sitting comfortably in a Cave of Sorrow, filled with shadows. You are warm and safe with nothing to fear. It is the right place and the right time to be sad. Watch the reflection of a candle flickering on the cave walls in this quiet for a number of minutes. Think of and honor your loss, trusting that the remembering and reflecting will shorten the time you need to stay here. Become aware of a Comforting Presence that understands. No words are necessary although you may hear reassurance. Imagine the tears of your regrets and sorrow drop into a pitcher sitting on the floor in front of you. When your sorrow feels heard, felt, and affirmed by this Presence, it is time to leave. You may return at other times until the need feels satisfied.
3. A thought experiment: On Releasing Anger

   If you are angry at the teachings of deprivation of pleasure, the belittling of natural human feelings and responses, or voices that said there was something wrong with your body as sexual, make a list of those voices you trusted but who caused you pain. After each name or situation, complete this sentence: "I am (angry/mad/regret/furious/enraged) because . . ." Now close your eyes and slowly count to ten. Imagine your emotion as hot energy. Move into a standing position if you are able and imagine standing on a cold mountain top. Read the list once again and blow the hot anger energy from your abdomen onto this ice and snow. Each slow breath extinguishes the fire inside and the tears at your feet melt into a calm, peaceful lake. If some things are not ready to be released, return and repeat the exercise until you arrive at peaceful acceptance.

The Kiss of Honesty

MEDITATION

One who gives an honest answer
gives a kiss on the lips.

Proverbs 24:26

Living honestly is a mark of a righteous person. Jesus was making this point when he commanded that our speech should be a simple "yes" or a simple "no" (Matthew 5:36–37). With this as the standard, no extravagant oaths are required to convince someone of one's honesty. In the parable of the seeds and sower, Jesus commends that we have "an honest and good heart and bear fruit with endurance" (Luke 8:15). While we like to think we are honest, there are times when dishonesty makes life easier. For example, when a relationship has hit a snag and someone needs to initiate a painful conversation—or worse yet, an argument—it can be easier to avoid it. Yet staying silent is dishonest. When one is dissatisfied with one's sexual experiences, or lack thereof, the honest action is to tell one's partner even at the risk of hurt feelings. After all, it could lead to positive change. There is no guarantee that honesty will be met with a mutually honest response, or that our need will be met. However, the silence that results from biting our tongues is never a mark of tolerance. It is more likely a form of cowardice.

Jesus's disciples were known to blurt out their opinions as when Peter disagreed with Jesus. He did not get the response he wanted (Mark 9:32–33). When we honestly state our needs or thoughts, we also run a risk of an unwanted response. But the choice to withhold our truth keeps the other person oblivious, leaving the impression that all is well. Not to disclose our deep dissatisfaction means concerns don't get talked out or resolved. And when no change occurs, we can become resentful or act out of spite.

To be sure, there is a time to speak and a time to stay silent (Ecclesiastes 3:7), but staying silent about a relational issue with an intimate partner because it seems safer is not wise. After all, an honest answer is to spread kisses among those around us. Let us, in our honesty, kiss the world, for that is exactly what the world needs.

One Who Kisses, we feel the kiss of creation, the kiss of life, the kiss of sensual touch, the kiss of love in our midst. Give us the courage to be honest in difficult conversations, honoring the feelings of our hearts with those we hold most dear. May we bring the gift of kisses from an open and honest heart.

REFLECTION

1. It may be most difficult to be honest with those who are closest to us. To disappoint or upset those in our closest circle runs the risk of the deepest pain. Make a list of those in your inner circle whose opinions matter most to you. Are you honest with them about how important they are in your life? If not, what are ways you can let them know? Choose one or more of those relationships and honestly express your gratitude.
2. Can you identify something in your most intimate relationship that is missing or that you would like to change? If so, why have you not broached the subject? What prevents you from being honest? What do you need to have the courage to approach the topic?
3. Stand in front of a mirror and watch as you purse your lips as if you were going to give a big kiss to yourself and say the following aloud. Smack your lips in a kiss after each line. Have fun with this.
   a. You are a good person. You look a little silly right now doing this though.
   b. You deserve to have your needs met—even if you look silly.
   c. Your opinion and ideas matter—speak up and I'll give you a kiss.
   d. I like you when you are honest with yourself.
   e. I like you even better when you are honest with others.
   f. You are a good person . . . but you do look a little silly right now.

Porn: Helpful or Harmful?

MEDITATION

Happy are those who observe justice,
who do righteousness at all times.

Psalm 106:3

There is some scientific research[30] on married couples that shows that when both partners have an interest in pornography, there is either positive benefit or no adverse effects on their marriage. In addition, pornography can serve as a release for sexual tension and support for sexual expression,[31] especially for single people. Despite the fact that there are situations in which erotic entertainment can satisfy curiosity, enhance one's own relationships, and loosen inhibitions, it remains a taboo in Western culture.

There are at least three reasons faithful people must carefully discern pornography use that are unrelated to any concerns with images of naked bodies or sex acts. The first two are when it is used to avoid talking to one's partner about unresolved intimacy issues,[32] and when it is used as sex education. All commercially made pornography is entertainment. Carefully staged and scripted actions, the display of emotions, and body positions are meant to be provocative and to entertain, not to reflect reality. And because it follows scripts based in stereotypes, sexism, racism, ableism, and ageism are perpetuated while the values of domination, violence, and gendered injustice are encouraged. The porn industry cannot begin to replace the value of comprehensive sex education that is grounded in science, reflects reality, and importantly, teaches the importance of consent. But the third reason for hesitation is not about porn use but porn production.

By definition, this multi-billion-dollar industry objectifies bodies. By paying for the "entertainment" of mainstream pornography, we support an industry with little interest in the bodily integrity of the performers or otherwise.[33] What are the working conditions? How are performers treated on and off the camera? Are young people being exploited or coerced, or is abuse or trafficking involved? We must use careful spiritual discernment lest we follow and perpetuate the world's disdain and violence toward bodies. The goal is to celebrate and respect all sexual bodies, naked or not.

O Naked One, thank you for your naked honesty about what you desire, the naked depth of your love, and your naked anger at injustice. We confess we distort the gift of our bodies instead of celebrating it. Teach us to be mindful of the world's distortions so we do not mindlessly conform.

REFLECTION

1. Some teach that fantasies are wrong by not reflecting loyalty to our partner. Yet outside the bedroom, fantasies from our imagination occur without such censorship. Think of the last sumptuous Thanksgiving buffet as an enjoyable fantasy that we want to re-experience. Our imagination is our friend, not enemy. It highlights delight and spins new possibilities, however unattainable. Make a list of individuals who have featured in your sexual fantasies. After reading each name say, "I am drooling over ________ ." At some point in the assignment, you may find that you begin to smile and giggle about the fun of this assignment. Write a prayer of gratitude for your fantasies.

2. For many, times of intimacy can include a sense that we are viewing ourselves from the outside. Therapists call this "spectatoring." Being absent from our bodies at such times may keep us from recalling unresolved conflict or unhealed traumas. When is the last time you engaged in "spectatoring" in intimate moments? What prompted it? What were you feeling? These may be issues you wish to address with a therapist.
3. Even outside the confines of intimacy, we may find we are not paying attention as a self-soothing numbness blocks our inner examination, preventing us from interacting with others or our environment. Sometimes that numbness is a grief response to bad news or difficult situations. If this happens to you, what circumstances led you to move toward numbness? What happens emotionally to make this a viable alternative? What prayer could express your experience and might lead you to choose a better response than numbing out? This may also be a conversation to hold with a trained professional.

The Porn Threat and Sexual Coercion

MEDITATION

There is no longer Jew or Greek; there is no longer slave or free; there is no longer male and female.

Galatians 3:28

There is a common though erroneous stereotype that men have a testosterone-driven (read: nearly uncontrollable) urge for orgasm that, if denied, will drive them to seek a sinful sexual release with pornography (thus proving the non-compliant wife is sexually insufficient and responsible for his "sin"). Marital sexual access is touted as a "merciful" drug. This stereotype assumes a gender discrepancy in sexual desire[34] with an unsupported biological justification that designates one gender as sexually dominant. For some, this stereotype is the foundation for a defense of and necessity for marriage, predetermined sex roles, a gender binary, and heterosexual normativity, granting power to the hapless male as the "victim" of his sexual need.

None of this reflects Jesus's teachings or life since he seems to have had little interest in marriage[35] or sexuality.[36] He focused on the inner person rather than enforcing gender roles. So how did women become responsible for men's sexual happiness even as their own need is, if not unexplored, then secondary? How did women become responsible for their husbands' "sin"? Oh yes, a Bible verse in Genesis 2:18 appears to relegate females to the support role of "helper."

A common traditional storytelling of the Creation is of a bereft and lonely male for whom the Creator fashions a woman as his assistant. But this story is not about a male needing a female.[37] The word *ezer*, translated as "helper," means companion or companion warrior.[38] An *ezer* is a social companion, as it's clearly stated, "It is not good for the [the man] to live alone." With equal power no assistant is needed, only mutual companionship. We have no responsibility for another's soul, sexual needs, or their sins.

One Who Sees Our Games, how tiresome we must be when we play games instead of being companions with one another. Help us take responsibility for our own actions and forgive us when we listen to gendered biases that discount and divide. Give us courage to stand in solidarity without taking responsibility for one another.

REFLECTION

1. In our social life we all have some legitimate responsibilities to others due to our familial and parenting roles. Make a list of the sexual responsibilities you carry because of gender. Circle the ones you would like to jettison.
2. Sometimes in enmeshed relationships it feels natural to carry responsibility for our equals' needs on physical, social, emotional, and spiritual levels. Identify any exhaustion you feel in carrying responsibility. Then write the following: "(Name), I release you into Divine hands that will care for you. I let go of my need to take responsibility for your decisions." Read this aloud, listening to the inner Responsible Voice that responds. Using the dominant and subdominant hand technique, write out the inner dialogue between your Responsible Voice and the Freeing Voice.
3. Taking care of others is often a justification for interference. Renaming it "love," we assume responsibility when the deeper need may be our own (for example, they may make us look bad, or they may abandon us). Re-examine your sense of responsibility for others and complete the sentence, "My need to keep being responsible is because . . ." What can you learn about yourself?

Sex as an Escape or Avoidance?

MEDITATION

For everything there is a season and
a time . . . to keep silent and a time to speak.

Ecclesiastes 3:1,7

Sometimes we look for a time to escape. We need a periodic escape from being constantly accessible and on call virtually around the clock. We escape through means as simple as vacations, or a fast from technology or as complex as a new job, moving to a different location, or a divorce. We may be startled to discover our life is filled with the same daily routines with the same people and realize it's time to shake things up, including in the bedroom. Sometimes we need to escape to some new ideas to escape sexual monotony. This motivation to escape is a push from our inner selves to address those needs that call to us. This kind of escaping may well reset the pleasure buttons of our lives.

But sometimes escaping is avoidance. We seek an external escape in our fear of vulnerable exposure to others and to ourselves, rather than laying out for ourselves and our partners what we *really* need or *really* want. The fear of naming what is missing from our lives or our relationships is the pull to escape risk, wanting to avoid fallout or the need to articulate what we don't want to acknowledge. Avoidance pulls us toward distractions that our intimate partners may detect, picking up the clues to our dis-ease. This kind of escape, whether through pornography or taking chances or acting out, is good neither for our mental health nor our relationships.

Unfortunately, many of us expect a faithful life to be a no-conflict zone: no arguments, no disagreements, only peaceful consensus with harmonious intimacy and unchanging relationships. But this is not what Jesus modeled. As we grow, learn, and mature, our goals and interests always shift. Therefore, relationship needs and intimate desires change as well. It is a truism that if nobody is talking about these changes then, over time, relationships degrade as unhappiness and resentment set in.

There is a reassuring wisdom in knowing that there is a time to keep silent and a time to speak, a time to escape into the pleasure that our inner wisdom desires and a time to avoid escaping into the distractions that camouflage our authentic desires. Our task is to ask ourselves if our silence is timely or if it is time to speak and bring our whole self into our intimate relationships.

Still Speaking and Silent One, sometimes we would prefer stage directions about when to speak up and when to stay silent, when to raise a ruckus and when it is wise to thoughtfully reconsider. Sometimes you speak loudly telling us to love whom you made us to be. And sometimes you are silent waiting for us to come to you to reveal your will. Help us be patient but also help us be real.

REFLECTION

1. Make a list of your favorite ways to escape when you need a break from pressure or need a change.

   Add a star by those ways of escaping that bring joy and ultimately reset your pleasure buttons.

   Draw a line through those strategies that you think are probably not so good for you, physically, socially, emotionally, or spiritually.

2. Identify anything you may be using as an escape to avoid conflict or delay a resolution and speak it aloud in private.
3. Identify one thing you would like to change about your sexual life, perhaps something you wish to try or explore or do differently. Identify the fear that keeps you from speaking this aloud. Then have a conversation with the One who silently awaits to hear and respond to your fears. Remember that this loving grace is always speaking to you in those scary places of sexuality.

Attention Heterosexual Men: Pleasure over Orgasm[39]

MEDITATION

Husbands should love their wives as their own bodies.
He who loves his wife loves himself.

Ephesians 5:28

We have a number of harmful myths in our culture—particularly in conservative Christian culture—that have the effect of ensuring that heterosexual men's sexual experiences will not be all that they could be. These can include: 1) Your sexual satisfaction is your partner's responsibility. 2) You can find self-worth and know if you are loved by whether you participate in penetrative sex. 3) Your partner's pleasure need not be your priority. The result? You may well trivialize or even negate your partner's hesitation or pushback. A partner's reluctance or hesitation may be stated, "I don't know," "Maybe," "I am not sure," "I changed my mind," "No," "It doesn't feel good." Any of these statements means there is not an enthusiastic invitation nor, perhaps, full consent. To proceed on the basis that sex is a man's right and a woman's responsibility is a direct violation of Jesus teaching to "Treat others as you wish to be treated" (Matthew 7:12). It contradicts the instructions that a wife's body is to be loved as one's own (Ephesians 5:28). The guiding principle here cannot be the male's sex drive but rather mutually loving action. When tied to partnered sexual expectations, it is never appropriate to use the language of "rights" or "responsibility." A marriage license is not to be taken as a once-for-always statement of consent. These misguided cultural myths may be why fewer than half of Christian evangelical women have regular orgasms although over sixty percent of non-evangelical and secular women do.[40] Husbands who demand and wives who comply are not only reducing pleasure—they are lowering the orgasm rate! When heterosexual men are not listening or if their partners are not being honest, this means that men will never have the satisfaction of being excellent pleasure-givers and women will never have the pleasure their bodies are capable of giving. Period.

To approach sexuality as a spiritual being is to keep the focus on maximizing mutual pleasure, with or without penetrative sex, with or without orgasm. In the sexual realm of intimacy, the spiritual requirement is marked by respect and honesty, love and consent. Mutual pleasure moves us toward the "get it on" experience that Marvin Gaye sang about and never, never settling for simply "getting off." We are made for, and we deserve, more than that.

Pleasure Giver, we admit we often overlook the small pleasures in life in our search for more and bigger. We confess it is tempting to look only to our own needs and desires. Forgive us when we make demands to others to fulfil our needs. Keep us honest. Keep us real.

REFLECTION

1. We experience pleasure and reduce sexual tension when we shift to giving and receiving sensual pleasure or focus on pleasuring the other person. It is to shift modes from body mechanics to relationship intimacy. Make a list of six pleasurable and sensual things your body loves that do not involve genitalia. Then note those you find difficult to acknowledge or ask for. Now ask yourself, why this is?
2. How comfortable are you with taking responsibility for your own self-pleasure? There is no teaching of Jesus that prohibits personal pleasure, so where was this learned? A parent? Church leader? Preacher? How might you say "Thanks, but no thanks" to that lesson, giving yourself permission to love your own body for the wonder it is?
3. Sometimes self-pleasure becomes problematic if the partner interprets this as reflecting an insufficiency on their part. Since this is most likely not the case, make a list of the sensual activities you engage in that do not require your partner's participation. Ask your partner to do the same and then broach the subject about mutual self-pleasure. If this is problematic, seek the advice of a qualified sex therapist to help you communicate with one another.[41]

Greatly Beloved Were You to Me

MEDITATION

Your love to me was wonderful.

2 Samuel 1:26

There is a Native American expression that says, "Listen to your heart, it knows." Because the heart has a mind of its own, so to speak, we are sometimes unexpectedly attracted to people we did not expect to fall in love with and who may not fit our attraction template. This might have been the case with King David. Even though he had seven wives and at least ten concubines (2 Samuel 15:16), he found he was more deeply attracted to Jonathan (2 Samuel 1:26). This relationship, fraught with family tensions and stress, meant the two of them met in secret and defied rules about familial allegiance. The Bible is not clear about nor particularly interested in the depth of the intimacy they shared, but it certainly does not condemn the strong love and devotion between the two men.

Perhaps King David would have understood the instruction from Sufi mystic and poet Rumi, who wrote, "Heart has plundered mind of its eloquence."[42] Yet this is when we can get into trouble. Do we act on the instincts of the heart and perhaps the hormones? What if following the heart means violating existing covenants or what if others will be hurt? What if others say your love is wrong or a sin? Then what? It is our mind that considers consequences and examines our motivations but does the heart want to listen? What if we shut out the heart and then live with heartbreak or regret wondering "what if?"

Before addressing the conundrum of ethical choices in the wise or foolish longings of the heart, there is an intermediate step: Gratitude. Should we not be grateful for love, wherever it occurs and in whatever form it takes? Surely being grateful for unexpected pleasure and joy in our lives is consistent with our life of faith. While sometimes our hearts may not be interested in common sense, rules, or consequences, it can be the seat of affirming and much-welcome messages: We are loved! To feel fully alive with our senses deeply engaged in an exhilarating and exuberant "Yes!" is to say yes to life and to love!

Then, after acknowledging the presence of gratitude, we can mindfully begin to make the important decisions.

God of Surprises of the heart, thank you for all serendipity that warms our hearts even when it confuses our brains. We are grateful for the delightful surprises of unexpected pleasure. When we are uncertain, keep us from denying the delight that feels like blessing, that rejoices in love without rushing to condemn, repress, or choose. Give us strength to consider our actions before making hurtful mistakes, and, when we inevitably do, thank you for understanding and forgiving.

REFLECTION

1. Body movement: Identify a current struggle that is a tug between your mind and your heart. Then stand if you are able and move into a posture that seems to fit the desire of your heart and a second posture that represents the mind. Now have a conversation between them by shifting your body into the heart and mind postures as they speak. Have this dialogue until they seem to agree on a wise solution.

2. The capacity to reason and to control our impulsivity is found in the mind, while the heart is viewed as the seat of our emotional needs. Spiritual wisdom happens when we listen to a dialogue between the two. Think about a time when you reasoned your way out of doing what your heart wanted. Then remember another time when you followed your heart without this mindful consideration first. How wise were those decisions or actions? And, if you have regret, is it because the dialogue between the heart and mind didn't occur? If so, repeat each line aloud three times.

- I am loved as I am, whole but not perfect.
- Mistakes and poor choices do not make me a bad person.
- I am whole but not perfect.
- I am loved.

The Spiritual Freedom to Design our Relationships

MEDITATION

All things are lawful for me,
but not all things are beneficial.

1 Corinthians 10:23

It is an amazing fiction that the Bible supports exclusive heterosexual monogamy as the form of marriage blessed by God. This was never the norm in Hebrew or Christian scriptures. Ruth, Jesus's ancestor, gave up her own family, culture, and homeland to cling to Naomi and pledged undying allegiance before she manipulated—that is, sexually seduced—a distant relative to marry her for their economic well-being. Jesus's ancestors include Rahab, a prostitute who is commended, and Tamar, who strategically had sex with her father-in-law for financial survival. Biblical custom required a man to serve as a surrogate husband for a sister-in-law if his brother died childless. In addition, when a man's wife didn't give birth to sons, he could simply add another wife or impregnate a slave. Moses had two wives, Abraham three, David had seven wives plus concubines, and, ever the political strategist, Solomon had seven hundred wives and three hundred concubines. Yet Jesus was not particularly interested in marriage, noting there would be no such practice in the afterlife (Matthew 22:30). So no, a happy nuclear family headed by a heterosexual cisgender couple is not a biblical model. Then what kinds of intimate relationships work for us?

We may seek egalitarian relationships rooted in mutuality and honesty; these values are consistent with self-love and loving others. With the freedom to control reproductive abilities, people in long-term intimate relationships may consider factors of economics and shared parenting. There is no scientific research[43] to support a family made up of only two adults of opposing genders. The apostle Paul writes of the freedom that we have in Christ and indicates all things are permissible to consider, even as not all things are beneficial (1 Corinthians 10:23). If there is mutually honest communication about sexual needs and desires, boundaries and consent, then by negotiating in good faith and being guided by love and respect for one another, all faithful Christians can choose the composition of their family in any way that enhances individual flourishing and nurtures mutual love and compassion. As people of faith, we are not bound by cultural legalism but are free to use the encompassing criteria that Jesus taught and modeled: the law of Love.

Liberating One, we know to live in love is a deep challenge even as the freedom of your liberating possibilities may scare us. Liberate us from cultural cages that mold us into the world's image. Nudge us out on the limb of faith to fly into your grace and your presence. May all our Spirit-led decisions be wise and beneficial.

REFLECTION

1. Traditionally, United States culture is heteronormative with the expectation of partners of opposite genders practicing exclusive and procreative monogamy. This is a cultural norm, not a biblical one. Identify three cultural rules that you wish did not exist or that you routinely violate.
2. Remembering that the Bible indicates God is more concerned about what is on the inside of a person than any outward attempts to show religiosity, what would societal rules about sexuality look like if love and pleasure were the priority in making the realm of God "on earth as it is in heaven"?
3. Read the following scenarios and rate them on a scale of one through five with one being "No way" and five being "Sounds like heaven to me."
   a. There are no sexual restrictions between mutually consenting adults in the privacy of their own home.
   b. Any number of adults who, regardless of marital status, commit to compassionately parent and rear a child to adulthood.
   c. Any number of people can be intimate partners without regard to race, gender or identity, or marital status without judgment.

d. Any mutually negotiated expression of sexuality that would bring pleasure to all involved in the privacy of one's home is affirmed.
e. Every community is required to spend tax dollars to create and make available pleasurable, sensual activities for all its citizens.
f. All people may choose to name their own gender, gender identity, and expression for themselves without judgment.

Note which of these fanciful cultural rules create the most anxiety or fear for you? Why?

Sacred Sex

MEDITATION

In my flesh I shall see God.

Job 19:26

The concept of sacred sex is known by those who adhere to Taoist principles from China, Tantric teaching from India, and the teachings within earth-centered religions such as Wicca. This understanding usually weaves spirituality with the physical, making the erotic experience a full-body spiritual connection. Although Christianity teaches that Jesus was both human and fully divine, we have no teaching similar to tantra. The historical Christian theological duality that separates the (so-called) impurity of the body from the purity of the spirit cannot lead to sacred sex. Yet our shared fleshly needs and sensual and spiritual desire for intimate connection reside in our bodies. To be seen, known, and loved in the deepest parts of ourselves is sacred and, if we lived unashamed, would perhaps mimic the experience of walking each evening in the sensual Garden of Earthly Delights with Love itself (Genesis 3:8).

We don't have to participate in this inherited war between our spirits and our bodies. Rather, by choosing partners wisely, the Christian understanding of faith, trust, and love in the Divine can move us with our beloveds into the lived experience known as sacred sex. To be open to the Sacred requires the courage to risk the loss of self that will explode all notions of separation. It is breathing in complete trust and receiving an abundant, nonjudgmental outpouring of Love that awaits. Faith. Trust. Love.

Accompanied by constant pain and suffering in his body, Job hit rock bottom in grief at his unimaginable losses. For him, for the Sacred to be real it had to make sense, not in his head, but in his frail body as well. He waited to know God through his own body (19:26). Like Job, we trust in the Sacred Goodness and Love that awaits us in our flesh. Nestled safely protected in the hand of Love itself, we can open ourselves to our erotic experiences and vulnerably risk unlatching the door of our psyche to the profound experience of being fully spiritual and fully sensual. Then all preconceptions fall away, revealing the illusion of separation and resurrecting instead a Oneness with all that is. Trusting, we lose our self in the eternity of the present moment and arrive in a transcendent space, however fleeting, of Divine Mystery beyond this frail human reality. It is to soar into the waiting palm of Love's hand and discover we are fully seen, completely known, and lavishly loved for our names are already written there (Isaiah 49:16).

Pleasure Designer, thank you for every juicy feeling of our bodies. Hold us safe as we learn to trust in ourselves, in our own goodness and our own worthiness so we will wisely choose relationships that are worthy of us. May every experience of pleasure remind us you are the Sacred Designer.

REFLECTION

1. Some fears have their origins in unresolved situations or past trauma. Acknowledging that some fears serve a good purpose while others do not, make a list to identify your hesitations about vulnerability during erotic times.
2. When have you been overwhelmed by unexpected Goodness, when a situation made you feel seen and loved, or when things seemed so unusual, wonderful, or so coincidental it seemed Divine intervention? These are sacred times. Relive those times in your mind, spending several minutes with each one. Remember the sights, sounds, smells, tastes, and touches of the experience.
3. To trust and take leaps of faith is to have confidence in your ability to keep yourself safe. Rate your ability from one to five for the following statements (one = "I can't trust myself" and five = "Very self-confident.")
    a. I can recognize honest and forthright people who are worthy of me.
    b. I recognize when I am in over my head and can and do ask for support.
    c. I can trust my heart and my head at the same time.
    d. When I make poor decisions, I try to understand so it doesn't happen again.
    e. I can see and avoid those who are manipulative.
    f. I know my weaknesses in relationship.

Reconnecting the Body and Spirit

MEDITATION

You have made them . . . lower than the angels;
you have crowned them with glory and honor.

Hebrews 2:7

The phrase "Be still and know that I am God" (Psalm 42:10) is usually (rightly) read as if the Divine were speaking. However, with a fully human and fully divine Jesus to reconnect our bodies with our spirits, let us instead prayerfully meditate on this verse in first person. It would read instead: *Be still and know that I am god.* Obviously, we are not God nor are we meant to be, and it would be inappropriate to think of ourselves as usurping the Divine or giving ourselves extraordinary powers. However, Genesis tells us as created beings we resemble the Creator (1:26) whether we are in the Garden or outside of it. Thus, all of humanity is spiritual and as sacred beings bears a reflection of the Sacred, even if and when we feel separated by guilt, fear, and shame. Even as we recognize our fragility and the transience of our bodies, we can still fully embrace the divine humanity space of being just a little lower than the angels (Hebrews 2:7).

Our resemblance to the Divine is made visible and experienced by others when we live into our Source and reflect this "godness" as our first ancestors did in the Garden of Earthly Delights. It is by reconnecting to our own inner divine state that the disconnection of our spirits and bodies can be healed. Our sole task is to remember whose we are, where we belong, and then begin to live and love like it.

Source of All Being, we long to be connected, to dive deep into your abundant Love, confident in our unity. So we say with St. Patrick: "Christ be with me, Christ within me, Christ behind me, Christ before me, Christ beside me, Christ to win me, Christ to comfort me and restore me, Christ beneath me, Christ above me, Christ in the hearts of all that love me, Christ in the mouth of friend and stranger."[44] *May it be so.*

REFLECTION

1. A meditation exercise[45]: To reconnect body and spirit, meditate on Psalm 46:10. Sit in a comfortable position, slow your breath, and repeat this verse as in the following ways:

   Be still and know that I am god.
   Be still and know that I am.
   Be still and know.
   Be still.
   Be.

   (Read the following aloud slowly and carefully. Keep your breath deep).

   Be still and know that I am god.

   Our Source is One, Life, Love, and Joy, and we are intimately connected. Can I recognize my own divinity, this "godness" within? Can I embrace and live into the "godness" inside my physical vessel holding my spirit, connecting me with Spirit?

   Be still and know.

   Knowing cannot be memorized nor stored in my head. Rather, I sit with the knowing that resides in my innermost being, usually at that center of my abdomen where the emotional intelligence lies. It is a knowing that connects with feeling satiated with Abundant Love and Unending Grace, knowing that leans into Goodness. Knowing says, "Ah-h-h-h." (Say "Ah-h-h-h" and as your breath pushes it out. Feel this knowing in your body.)

Be still

In stillness, I become aware of the high traffic patterns of the world's values that control our lives, disturb our spirits, and mold and deform us into the world's image. It separates me from my Source. Be still. I can settle into a quiet knowing: there is something better. Someone calls me to my best and my highest self when I slow down and be still. In stillness sacred whispers are heard for when, where, and how to love in my body. Listen.

Be.

The invitation is to be the sacred potential that Jesus understood. Be who I am at my core: One with all of humanity, a smattering of atoms of stardust that emanate throughout our reflections toward all that we touch. Be Love. Be Joy. Be Hope. Be connected to all that is.

Ultimately, to "be," to "be still," and to "be still and know" is to simply be who God made us to be—not Gods, but godly; not perfect, but faithful.

And it is all good. It is very good.

May the Holiness above, beyond, around, and inside us radiate outward to all we encounter. May the Sacred hold us as One and dissolve all needless boundaries of division. And may we be witnesses to the holy gift of life, in these bodies.

Afterword:
In Closing, There is No Closure

God has revealed to us through the Spirit,
for the Spirit searches everything, even the depths
of God . . . Now we have received not the spirit
of the world but the Spirit that is from God, so that we
may understand the gifts bestowed on us by God.

1 Corinthians 2:10, 12

Learning to accept that all of our selves are made in the image of God is daunting; the task of weeding out body-negativity from the entrenched traditions of Christian teaching is herculean. It is also true that as we become more body-positive, it revolutionizes our self-image and self-definition as well as our capability for intimacy. This shift has the potential to upend our relationships, hopefully for the better, though there are no guarantees. It also changes our understanding of other bodies, particularly those whom sexual teachings may have marginalized or ostracized due to gender, orientation, age, being differently-abled, or non-white or poor. Accepting human unity in diversity requires our mutual responsibility to live into the reality of the "Beloved Community," as Martin Luther King, Jr spoke of it, and to do this "on earth as it is in heaven," as Jesus prayed.

The Spirit moves us out of the safe and familiar and into places we did not expect to go, with concepts and understandings that we may not, at first, even appreciate. When the Spirit calls, sometimes it means we must leave a community that we love. It may mean enforcing boundaries and refusing to give consent to what others insist upon. Sometimes it requires that we remove ourselves from toxic relationships or that we re-examine our image and ideas of God. Spirit always surprises and surprises are not always welcome. Old habits of thinking are hard to give up. For when the Spirit speaks, our ego is not so easily silenced. Rather, it will work all the harder to maintain control, refusing to give up its throne. In addition, the painful memories and destructive lessons that may remain stored in our bodies need time to be first, recognized, and then healed. Walking the spiritual path is never easy.

But does assuming a body-positive Christianity that rejoices in pleasure and emphasizes the goodness and potential of the enfleshed human family negate the idea of sin? No, it does not. Sin is whatever separates us from our Divine Source. It is anything that misses the mark of righteous living. When we are separated from—or have not yet discovered—the "godness" within us, we can and do act out of ignorance, ego, or our own woundedness. When this happens, we reveal the harm of which we are capable individually and systemically. In truth, as we move toward a body-positive faith, the many, many ways we fall short of our "godness" become more apparent. There are times we do not treasure the gift and beauty of our own bodies nor the precious bodies of others.

On this spiritual journey of reconnecting our body and spirit, Wisdom reveals an important lesson: It is almost, but not yet. The vision of what could be if we could see the Spirit of God in each and every body we meet is breathtaking and yet out of the reach of our imperfect humanity. We will never fully arrive, yet we stay on the journey by faith. We may never fully recover from our spiritual and sexual wounding, yet we keep seeking healing from the Spirit that is of God. Our goal is to seek an understanding of "the gifts bestowed on us from God" (1 Corinthians 2:10–12).

It should be apparent by now that faith is not about assenting to intellectual beliefs or obeying religious teaching, nor is it about following external rules about who we are or should be and how we are to behave sexually as people of faith. Rather, faith is the ongoing movement toward embracing the Divine Source within ourselves. It is the movement toward the Source from which we came, the Creative Force that made us in its own image. Faith keeps us moving forward even when everything around us may tell us to quit and conform. Even when we do not sense solid ground beneath our feet, still, we keep walking. The Spirit from God keeps us moving "toward the prize of the heavenly call" (Philippians 3:14).

I had a wise Christian grandma who was a deep thinker. Born and raised in the rural parts of the Midwest, she became a farmer's wife without ever having graduated from high school. Yet in her quiet manner, she had gone beyond her church's easy answers and asked the hard and deep philosophical questions of life's meaning and purpose. I admired her quiet, questioning spirit that reflected wisdom and maturity. When I was in my mid-thirties and wrestling with my own spiritual dilemmas, I asked her directly if we ever actually get it right. I asked, "Do we ever arrive at some plateau of understanding and finally get it?" I assumed that by the age of ninety-five, she would know. But she responded very quickly, "Oh, goodness! No! Not at all. I am still working on it!"

We do not live in the Garden of Eden, but it is there that we belong. We are indeed separated from the One who keeps calling us back home, back to ourselves, back to our bodies. Thus, the movement of the Spirit is never truly forward but instead is a return to that which we have forgotten. It is a return to Love. The Spirit calls us. Can we hear it? The journey of faith is to move toward our

Source, back to the Garden where intimacy resides and where no one is ashamed, where the sensual is everywhere apparent, honored, and appreciated, where all of creation is maintained and cared for, and where we, in our bodies, are a part of the creation and intimately absorbed into the Creator who is our Divine Source.

That is the gift bestowed on us. And that is the prize of the heavenly call: to embody the Jesus who, as God-in-the-flesh, was fully human and fully divine and who showed us how to be spiritual in these human bodies. The Body of Christ is being called to return home, to come back to where we belong.

May we, together, come home to our beautiful sexual bodies—unashamed.

Appendix

SUGGESTED SEX-POSITIVE CHRISTIAN RESOURCES

I have included some authors who may or may not teach specifically about sexuality but whose writings focus on spiritual liberation. They critique harmful and rigid Christianity and understand the importance of using the intersections of multiple spiritual resources in our personal stories to inform our faith.

Purity Culture

Pure: Inside the Evangelical Movement and How I Broke Free (Atria 2018) by Linda Kay Klein is a recounting of Klein's experience with the purity culture in her church as well as the stories of many young women from her former youth group who were coping with the same shame-induced issues. This is a recounting of a twelve-year quest to facilitate her own healing and discover a new way to reconcile sexuality and spirituality.

#ChurchToo: How Purity Culture Upholds Abuse and How to Find Healing (Broadleaf Books 2021) by Emily Joy Allison, who started #ChurchToo. The book reveals the church's sexual dysfunction, which allows sexualized violence in those religious spaces that become uniquely traumatizing. She examines how there are many paths for victims of assault to heal from religiously instilled sexual shame, secrecy, and control to live full, free, healthy lives.

See Me Naked: Stories of Sexual Exile in American Christianity (Beacon Press 2011) by Amy Frykholm revolves around the stories of nine American Protestants at the intimate intersection of sexuality and spirituality as they maneuver through indictments of, or blind allegiance to, Christian cultures in their lives. She addresses how some American Christians can access their spiritual tradition and heal the divide between religion and sexuality.

The Great Sex Rescue: The Lies You've Been Taught and How to Recover What God Intended by Sheila Wray Gregoire, Rebecca Gregoire Lindenbach, and Joanna Sawatsky (Baker Books 2021) is based on a study of over twenty thousand women that exposes what happens when Christian households are taught sex negativity that is destructive for relationships. The authors also offer correctives to this church culture.

Living in Sin: A Bishop Rethinks Sexuality (HarperCollins 1990) by John Shelby Spong, a well-known and widely published Episcopal bishop, proposes a pastoral response to the changing sexual realities of the modern world. Using scripture and history, he proposes a moral vision to empower the church with inclusive teaching about relationships that are equal, loving, and nonexploitative.

Biblical Studies

Misquoting Jesus: The Story Behind Who Changed the Bible and Why (HarperCollins 2007) by Bart Ehrman, a biblical scholar who makes the case that many widely held beliefs about the divinity of Jesus, the Trinity, and the divine origins of the Bible are actually the results of alterations by scribes, both intentional and accidental.

God and Sex (Twelve 2011) by Michael Coogan, is a scholar of Old Testament scriptures who writes of what scripture says about sex and how contemporary understandings of those writings frequently misunderstand or misrepresent them. Coogan explores the language and social world of the Bible, showing how much innuendo and euphemism is at play and illuminating the sexuality of biblical figures as well as God.

Sex Texts from the Bible: Selections Annotated and Explained (Skylight Paths, 2007) by Teresa Hornsby is a short text that demystifies the Bible by explaining each key biblical text about sexuality and how to read it inclusively and critically. It bridges the divide between biblical authority and current views of gender roles, marriage, sexual orientation, virginity, lust, and sexual pleasure.

Unprotected Texts: The Surprising Biblical Contradictions about Sexuality (HarperCollins, 2012) by Jennifer Wright Knust, an academic theologian, thoroughly investigates the many sexuality related passages of scripture and concludes that, given the wide discrepancies and contradictions in the Bible, absolutist conclusions are simply not supported and cannot be justified.

The Making of Biblical Womanhood: How the Subjugation of Women Became Gospel Truth (Brazos Press 2021) by Beth Allison Barr is about an evangelical woman who returns to church history—ancient, medieval, and modern times - to show how the belief of women's roles is not divinely ordained but a product of human civilization that continues to creep into church teaching.

Sexual Liberation: The Scandal of Christendom (Praeger 2007) by Raymond Lawrence is an accounting of how the early Jesus movement and the morality of Greco-Roman culture and empire intersected and how Christianity's moral code was reshaped when Constantine adopted Christianity as the imperial religion. Later, key figures of the Middle Ages promoted a religion that sought to obliterate sexual pleasure.

Spiritual Discernment of Sexuality

Damaged Goods (Jericho Books 2015) by Dianna Anderson is a personal account of how she moved from the strictness of the Purity Culture stigma and media pressures and how she reconciles scripture and culture using common sense to come out the other side.

Faith Unraveled: How a Girl Who Knew All the Answers Learned to Ask Questions (Zondervan 2014) by Rachel Held Evans is only one of Held Evan's books detailing her spiritual journey from certainty to doubt to faith as she shifts away from false fundamentals to move toward trust in a God who is not put off by our questions.

Femmevangelical: The Modern Girl's Guide to the Good News by Jennifer D. Crumpton (Chalice Press 2015) is all about finding good news in the gospel of Jesus with an emphasis on discovering a different reality of equality, freedom, and wholeness.

This Here Flesh: Spirituality, Liberation, and the Stories That Make Us (Convergent Books 2022) by Cole Arthur Riley, a creator of Black Liturgies, uses stories of three generations of her family to find the sacred deep inside. In seeking healing and wholeness, she focuses on spiritual stories of embodiment to learn to survive by asking the provocative question, "How can spirituality not silence the body?"

Sensuous Spirituality: Out From Fundamentalism by Virginia Ramey Mollenkott (The Pilgrim Press 2008) integrates sexuality and spirituality, social activism and personal peace. Using "generic feminine" language Mollenkott discusses the Bible, the erotic, the gender continuum, our images of God, and family-church parallels.

Sensual Faith: The Art of Coming Home to Your Body by Lyvonne Briggs (Convergent Books 2023) teaches radical self-hospitality and centers the traditions of West African spirituality by focusing on pleasure rather than shame to help women practice spiritual wellness.

Sexual Ethics

Erotic Justice: A Liberating Ethic for Justice (Westminster John Knox 1996) by Marvin Ellison, a pioneer in contemporary rethinking in Christianity about sexuality and sexual ethics, demonstrates a liberating Christian ethic that goes beyond the historical patriarchal view.

Making Love Just: Sexual Ethics for Perplexing Times (Fortress Press, 2012) by Marvin Ellison uses provocative real-life scenarios to shift conventional thinking based on rule-based sexual morality to show how redrawing the sexual map helps to transcend fear and shame. He applies a relationally focused ethical framework grounded in justice to issues such as premarital and extramarital sex, marriage and divorce, homosexuality, contraception, abortion, spousal abuse, and sex education.

Body, Sex and Pleasure, Reconstructing Christian Sexual Ethics (The Pilgrim Press 1995) by Christine Gudorf, a theologian and ethicist, grounds her work in scripture and encourages us to drop the mind/body dualism and do justice as we re-center our sexual ethics.

Liberating Sexuality: Justice between the Sheets (Chalice Press 2016) by Miguel De La Torre, a Christian ethicist who works at the intersection of race, class, sexuality, and gender. The book tackles controversial topics such as an androgynous Jesus, ethical S&M, and confronting racism in one's sexual preferences.

A Lily Among the Thorns: Imagining a New Christian Sexuality (Jossey Bass 2007) by theologian Miguel De La Torre promotes a just and biblically based sexual ethic by reading the Bible from the viewpoint of those who have been marginalized. He shows how the church's traditionally negative attitudes toward sex in general, and especially toward women, people of color, and sexual minorities, have made it difficult to foster intimacy, vulnerability, and openness between loving partners.

Exploring the intersections of race, class, gender, sexual orientation

Sisters in the Wilderness: The Challenge of Womanist God-Talk (Orbis 2013) by Delores Williams is a classic text that uses stories of biblical women to understand the struggles of African-American women at the intersection of race, sex, and class.

A Troubling in My Soul: Womanist Perspectives on Evil and Suffering (Orbis Books 1993) edited by Emilie Townes offers a variety of well-known and honored womanist theologians who show the shortcomings of traditional, feminist, and Black theologies in dealing with the problem of evil. Though not specifically about sexuality, these essays highlight the ways in which race, gender, and class intersect and contribute to suffering.

Just a Sister Away: A Womanist Vision of Women's Relationships in the Bible, (Walk Worthy Press 2007) by author and scholar. Renita Weems is written primarily with African American women in mind, as she explores a variety of women in scripture through a liberating lens of race and gender. An excellent source for book discussion groups.

White Women's Christ and Black Women's Jesus: Feminist Christology and Womanist Response (Scholar's Press 1989) by Jacqueline Grant is a critique of the way the Jesus story gets told using the lens of race, class, and gender and suggests that we need to look to the life experiences of women of color to more adequately understand who Jesus was and is.

Rainbow Theology: Bridging Race, Sexuality, and Spirit (Church Publishing 2013) by Patrick S. Cheng, who identifies as a gay Asian Christian theologian, explores the aspects of queerness that both inform and liberate Christianity from its white privilege and its sex-negative, homophobic theological position.

Sexuality and the Black Church: A Womanist Perspective (Orbis Books 1999) by Episcopal priest and womanist theologian Kelly Brown Douglas tackles the issues of sex negativity and the taboos within the Black church, most especially toward homosexuality, and correlates this to the history of white supremacy.

Is the Homosexual my Neighbor? Revised and Updated: Positive Christian Response (Harper One 1994) by Letha Dawson Scanzoni and Virginia Ramey Mollenkott is a revolutionary classic that looks at homosexuality from scientific, psychological, and biblical perspectives using the lens of justice and has been updated to discuss issues such as AIDS and genetic research.

Coming Out as Sacrament (Westminster, John Knox 1998) by Chris Glaser is an openly gay pastor and public activist for whom coming out is an act of vulnerability, similar to a sacrificial offering of ancient times, that invokes God's presence and reconciliation. Like other sacraments, coming out can serve as a means of grace and provide the experience of God's unconditional love.

OtherWise Christian: A Guidebook for Transgender Liberation (OtherWise Academy 2019) by Mx Chris Paige is scholarly, yet accessible. The book takes the Bible seriously, even as it presents new vocabulary to connect modern transgender (and intersex) identities with gender non-conforming themes in the Christian Bible. It pushes against a restrictive gender ideology that is aligned with empire, white supremacy, and Christian supremacy to connect modern transgender (and intersex) identities with gender non-conforming themes in the Christian Bible.

Christian Faith and Gender Identity: An OtherWise Reflection Guide (OtherWise Reflection Guides Book 1 2019) by Mx Chris Paige is a seven-day devotion guide that draws on texts from Genesis, Exodus, Matthew, John, Acts, and Galatians to introduce concepts around gender identity for transgender, intersex, and OtherWise-gendered Christians and their allies.

Further Resources for Healing Body Injustice

Journal of Radical Permission: A Daily Guide for Following Your Soul's Calling Diary by adrienne maree brown and Sonya Renee Taylor (Berrett-Koehler Publishers 2022). This journal is designed to free us to live our purpose and gives permission to love oneself. It is based on the philosophies of radical self-love and pleasure activism by two best-selling authors.

The Body is Not an Apology Workbook: Tools for Living Radical Self-Love (Berrett-Koehler Publishers 2021) by Sonya Renee Taylor is an action guide with tools and structured frameworks. It offers radical self-love as the balm to heal the wounds inflicted by violent systems. The poet and renowned activist invites us to deepen the radical self-love journey and dismantle body shame and celebrate our collective, enduring strength.

Pleasure Activism: The Politics of Feeling Good (AK Press 2019) by adrienne maree brown has assembled writers who address a wide array of subjects—from sex work to climate change, from race and gender to sex and drugs, but each one believes that the politics of healing and happiness can and is changing the world.

Care Work: Dreaming Disability Justice (Arsenal Pulp Press 2018) by Leah Lakshmi Piepzna-Samarasinha explores the realities of the disability justice movement and celebrates radical love and the work of sick and disabled queer/people of color who are building power and community so that no one is left behind. It is a tool kit for those who want to build radically resilient and sustainable communities of liberation.

My Body Is Not a Prayer Request: Disability Justice in the Church (Brazos 2022) by Amy Kenny argues that the church must start treating disabled people with more than a miraculous cure narrative but are to be included as full members of the body of Christ. And, as such, they have much more to offer the church if it would begin to learn from their embodied experiences.

How Ableism Fuels Racism: Dismantling the Hierarchy of Bodies in the Church (Brazos Press 2024) by Lamar Hardwick, who, as a Black autistic pastor and disability scholar, believes that it is ableism and disability discrimination that are the root causes of racial bias and injustice in American culture and in the church.

On the Spectrum: Autism, Faith, and the Gifts of Neurodiversity (Brazos Press 2021) by Daniel Bowman, Jr., is a poet and professor who was diagnosed as autistic at the age of thirty-five. Bowman debunks myths about autism and shows authentic ways to love one's neighbors, including those autistic neighbors, who are fearfully and wonderfully, if differently, made.

Movements for Liberation of the Body

Our Own Voice is a reproductive justice newsletter of a collective of US organizations led by Black women who understand that their experiences of racism, sexism, and classism are inseparable. Their human rights perspective incorporates the intersections of race, gender, class, sexual orientation, and gender identity with the impacts of economics, politics, and culture.

The Poor People's Campaign is a grassroots multi-racial and non-violent campaign with a primary focus on the moral issues of how our society treats the poor, those on the margins, women, LGBTQIA2S+ folks, workers, immigrants, the disabled, and the sick. The group works for equal protection under the law and the desire for peace, love, and harmony within and among nations.

Transfaith is a national non-profit led by transgender people that is multi-tradition, multi-racial, multi-gender, and multi-generational. The group works to support transgender spiritual/cultural workers and their leadership in community.

Soulforce works to end religious and political oppression of LGBTQI people by breaking open the ideologies of Christian supremacy and healing our communities' spirits of Spiritual Violence.

Woodhull Freedom Foundation works to fight censorship, eliminate discrimination based on gender, sexual identity, or family form, and protects the right to engage in consensual sexual activity and expression.

Video Resources:

Doing Time in the No Mo Homo Half Way House: How I Survived the Ex-Gay Movement by Peterson Toscano is a performance of a one-man show in which the performer reveals his exposure to the ex-gay movement from which he successfully graduated but remained gay. It is silly and very serious.

Transfigurations: Transgressing Gender in the Bible is a provocative video written, produced, and performed by activist Peterson Toscano, who has unearthed biblical stories of gender diverse people in scripture. It is ground-breaking, genre-bending, gender-blending biblical scholarship.

Sex is Good by Beverly Dale is an eight-part video series on YouTube that covers a variety of sexual topics. Meant to be used as a discussion starter, each short video contains scriptural references.

Acknowledgments

We are all deeply influenced by those before us and around us—some we know and others we do not. I have been touched and blessed by so many who have encouraged and challenged me on my spiritual path toward wholeness. My work has been heavily influenced by the theological scholarship of those who were on the path before me: the late Dr. Virginia Ramey Mollenkott, Dr. James B. Nelson, Dr. Robin Scroggs, Dr. Rosemary Radford Ruether, and Dr. James Cone. I am particularly indebted to theologians Carter Heyward, Rita Nakashima Brock, Kelly Brown Douglas, Laurel Schneider, Marvin Ellison, and Miguel de la Torre.

There have been younger women like Linda Kay Klein whose stories of the purity culture serve as the impetus to push toward the vision of a body-positive Christianity. These include the voices of Rachel Keller, Alexandra Day, Hannah Scheri Horton, Onika Henry, Chesla Nickelson, members of the Board of the Incarnation Institute for Sex & Faith, and each of the IISF trainees who have validated the importance of this work.

My writer's group that has met regularly for over a decade includes Rev. Elizabeth Ellis, Amy Mann, and Laurie Perman, each of whom shared important insights and suggestions as well as enthusiastic support. We should all be so lucky to have friends like Rev. Dr. Susan Minasian and Andrea Durham who, each in their own way, have been witness to and assisted my own movement into my calling, and Rev. Dr. Lacette Cross, who joined me as a complementary partner and colleague on this journey.

And to keep all anxiety and panic at bay, my in-house promoter, fan, and, fortunately, volunteer editor, Dr. Lawrence Souder, has always known the right words to say to bring me back to my center, back to where Spirit is. I am truly blessed.

ENDNOTES

1. From the one-woman show titled "An Irreverent Journey from Egg-beaters to Vibrators," written and produced by Beverly Dale.

2. There seems to be two separate trees, the Tree of Life and the Tree of the Knowledge of Good and Evil (2:9, 2:17, 3:29). It appears their eyes were opened when they chose knowledge. Then they could see the separation of who they were and who the Creator was/is.

3. See Scott Page, *The Diversity Bonus: How Great Teams Pay Off in the Knowledge Economy* (Princeton: Princeton University Press, 2019).

4. This exercise of using our non-dominant hand allows both parts of our brain to become activated helping us think differently and more creatively. This is elaborated in Lucia Capacchione, *The Creative Journal: The Art of Finding Yourself* (Athens, OH: Ohio University Press, 2015).

5. This phrase comes from the fourteenth-century Christian mystic, St. Julian of Norwich writing during the time of the Black Plague and deep social unrest in Europe. "All is well. And all will be well and all manner of things will be well."

6. Special thanks to Jonathan Poletti for pointing out the scholarship of this problematic text in "8 Things that Christians Say that just Ain't True," *Medium*, March 17, 2021, https://link.medium.com/6LHkNKilTib.

7. Figures are from 2021 in "US Weight Control and Diet Market," *Global Newswire*, (March 2023).

8. The New Revised Standard version spells her name as Jael although Hebrew does not have a "J." Yael is the transliteration of what this woman's name sounds like in Hebrew.

9. This subtle or not-so-subtle shade in this resemblance is found in white, heterosexual cisgender men in particular.

10. This exercise is part of Betty Martin's "Wheel of Consent" in which she specifically focuses on the practice of giving sexual consent. It can be found here: https://bettymartin.org/videos/.

11. By the author, unpublished.

12. This is reported by John Chrysostom, an early church father in the fifth century. Robin M. Jensen reported this in *Baptismal Imagery in Early Christianity, Ritual, Visual and Theological Dimensions* (Grand Rapids, MI: Baker Academic, 2012).

13. Since a community's survival depended on the grain storage of the harvest, snakes were valued for the protection they gave in eating the vermin that would hide there. Unlike the duplicitous snake in the monotheistic version of Genesis, these snakes were revered.

14. Harriet Lutzky, "Shadday as a Goddess Epithet," *Vetus Testamentum*, January 1998, 15–36.

15. Miguel A. de la Torre, *Liberating Sexuality, Justice Between the Sheets* (St. Louis: Chalice, 2016).

16. See Jesus's parable of the story known as "The Prodigal Son," Luke 15:11–32.

17. See Meditation "The Ethics of Apostle Paul-Conscience."

18. Carol Gilligan, and Naomi Snider, *Why Does Patriarchy Persist?* (New York: Wiley, 2018).

19. Naydeline Mejia and Sha Ravine Spencer, "What You Need to Know About The CROWN Act—And How It Impacts Black Women,", January 17, 2023, https://www.shape.com/lifestyle/beauty-style/black-women-natural-hair-experiences-at-work. (The research came from Dove, the soap company.)

20. By the author, unpublished.

21. See Meditation on "Deceit and the Sunglasses Test" for a clarification on the traditional English translation of this verse.

22. Jessica Valenti, *The Purity Myth: How America's Obsession with Virginity is Hurting Young Women* (Berkeley: Seal, 2009).

23. For further elaboration see Crystal Byrd Farmer, "The Triangle of Consent," *COMMUNITIES: Life in Cooperative Culture* 183 (Summer 2019): 30–31.

24. This is usually incorrectly translated as "your love is sweeter than wine." The correct translation is specifically and erotically sexual. See Hebrew scholar David Carr's book The Erotic Word: Sexuality, Spirituality, and the Bible (Oxford: Oxford University Press, 2005).

25. Ibid.

26. These are described in more detail in Gary Chapman, *The 5 Love Languages: How to Express the Heartfelt Commitment to Your Mate* (Chicago: Northfield Publishing, 1992).

27. However, this is often skewed by gender in our society, with women being socialized to engage in self-denial for the sake of others in general and men in particular.

28. Ola W. Barnett, Tomas E. Martinez, and Brendon W. Bluestein, "Jealousy and Romantic Attachment in Maritally Violent and Nonviolent Men," *Journal of Interpersonal Violence* 10, no. 4 (1995): 473–86; Gary L. Hansen, "Perceived Threats and Marital Jealousy," *Social Psychology Quarterly* 48, no. 3 (1985): 262–68.

29. *Codependent No More, How to Stop Controlling Others and Start Caring For Yourself*, by Melody Beattie

30. Joshua B. Grubbs, Julie J. Exline, Kenneth I. Pargament, Fred Volk, and Matthew J. Lindberg, "Internet Pornography Use, Perceived Addiction, and Religious/Spiritual Struggles," *Archives of Sexual Behavior*, 46, no. 6 (2017): 1733–45.

31. Beáta B the, István Tóth-Király, Nóra Bella, Marc N Potenza, Zsolt Demetrovics, and Gábor Orosz, "Why Do People Watch Pornography? The Motivational Basis of Pornography Use," *Psychology of Addictive Behavior* 35, no. 2 (2021): 172–86.

32. See Meditation "Sex as an Escape."

33. There are a minority of producers and directors of pornography who place a priority on ensuring their product has no exploitation. Ethical pornography celebrates sexual diversity, respects the performers, and has good working conditions. And no exploitation. See "How to find Ethical Porn," https://mashable.com/article/how-to-choose-ethical-porn or Ethical Porn Sites, https://ethicalpornsites.com/.

34. This gender myth is not borne out by social science research. Rather, stimuli are needed but the responses are different and we are aroused differently. Further, there is a wider variety of disruptions for women, such as child-bearing and post-partum issues and unequal burden of child care responsibilities, all external factors that impact women more than men.

35. He said there would be none in heaven. Matthew 22:30.

36. The single exception was an admonishment not to covet (poorly translated as lust) after another man's wife or, according to the Ten Commandments, his cows (Matthew 5:28, Exodus 20:17, Deuteronomy 5:21).

37. This was first exhaustively argued by the respected and renowned Hebrew scholar Phyllis Trible, *God and the Rhetoric of Sexuality* (Philadelphia: Fortress, 1978).

38. For example, God is the "help meet" or helper in a variety of Psalms 20:2, 33:20, 70:5, 115:9 and 11, 124:8.

39. Recognizing that our culture gives very specific messages—usually destructive—to gendered people to enforce a framework of domination that always gives some more power than others, it is important that we are sympathetic to the difficulties and harm that this creates both for ourselves and others. So while this meditation is particularly focused on heterosexual men, all readers are advised to read and think on these things.

40. Sheila Wray, Rebecca Gregoire Lindenbach, and Joanna Swatsky, *The Great Sex Rescue: The Lies You've Been Taught and How to Recover What God Intended* (Grand Rapids, MI: Baker, 2021)

41. Not all professional counselors or therapists have academic training in sexuality and sexual health research. Look for a professional with certification from the American Association of Sex Educators, Counselors and Therapists (AASECT). In addition, some trained professionals have received additional faith-based training in sexuality and Christianity from the Incarnation Institute for Sex & Faith (IISF).

42. Coleman Barks, *Rumi, The Book of Love: Poems of Ecstasy and Longing* (New York: HarperCollins, 2005), 36.

43. Timothy J. Biblarz, "How Does the Gender of Parents Matter?" *Journal of Marriage and Family* 72, no. 1 (2010): 3–22.

44. St. Patrick's Breastplate or *The Lorica (Cry of the Deer)*, Daily Prayers, https://www.daily-prayers.org/angels-and-saints/prayers-of-saint-patrick-of-ireland/.

45. The psalm in this exercise can be enhanced musically by using the rendition of a song titled, "Be (Still and Know That I Am God)" recorded by musicians Trish and Richard Bruxvoort-Colligan.